an Exeter Boyhood

Frank Retter

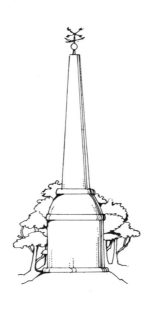

OBELISK PUBLICATIONS

preface

Many people will remember Mr Retter as the Senior Mathematics Teacher at Torquay Grammar School where he taught from 1947 until his retirement in 1965. Personally my recollecticn, triggered by this book, is of his small corner shop in Magdalen Sreet, Exeter where as a child I used to rummage through sweet cigarette packets searching for picture cards of my favourite soccer teams. Reading through this fascinating little book it brought memories flooding back to me as it no doubt will to all Exonians. I am sure it will be just as interesting to people who are newcomers to the area and will give them an invaluable insight into the day-to-day history of Exeter as it was early this century.

Chips Barber.

Chips Barber

*First published in 1984
by Obelisk Publications,
22 Causey Gardens, Pinhoe, Exeter, Devon.
Designed and Typeset by Sally Barber*

Cover Illustrations by Jane Reynolds

Contents

The new Exe Bridge - 1905

W Brock & Co, Fore St and North Street

Life in St Thomas

My first memories of Exeter date from about 1906 and are centred around Church Road in St Thomas where my parents, after their marriage in 1900, ran a small business. My mother, previous to her marriage, had been Manageress of Channings Dairy in Bedford Circus; my father had been employed as a butcher, so it was natural that this first joint effort should have consisted of the unusual mixture of these two trades. One side of the shop was devoted to the sale of milk, butter and cream and the other side featured the sale of meat, sausages and so on. I remember the heavy, solid wooden block, some four foot square and nearly six inches thick and standing on four very stout legs about eighteen inches in length, on which were arranged the chopper, saw and knives common to the butcher's trade.

At the age of three I was sent to a little private school, the Beaufort School for Girls (and Young Gentlemen). It was run by three "Piggs": Miss Carrington Pigg, Miss Ethel Pigg and their father. One cannot imagine anyone today having the temerity to start a school when handicapped by such names - they would surely be changed by way of Porker, probably to Parker - but in those days their names passed without comment or undue hilarity.

This school was situated in Cowick Street, directly opposite St Thomas Church and next door to the St Thomas Fire Station. This had housed a horse-drawn engine - I seem to recall that it turned out to a fire at Ide sometime in those very early years - but I remember only the new "Merryweather" motor fire-engine which replaced the earlier one.

The side door of the school was actually just inside St Thomas Pleasure Ground. We sat normally at suitably small desks in the carpetless front room on the first floor and our early lessons were on slates using lead

The former Fire Station and the Beaufort School in St Thomas

pencils. There were about ten boys - three, four or five year olds - in that one group and the only lesson I can recall related to behaviour outside the premises. The desks were pushed to one side, we were lined up and then instructed to walk in a circle round and round the room, all of us wearing caps: each time we passed Miss Carrington's desk we had to raise our caps and say "Good morning, Miss Pigg". This lesson was repeated daily until it was clear that we knew exactly what to do should we pass a lady in the street. Mr Pigg was clearly an unqualified addition to the staff: he was

6

often seen sitting on the landing at a side window, armed with a large cardboard clockface, with a group of small children clustered round him learning the secrets of time-telling.

The short journey from Church Road to the school was usually unescorted, since there was very little traffic to cause anxiety to parents. The horse-drawn trams which had made their appearance in 1882 had given way to electric trams in 1905; they were still much of an innovation when I started school in 1906. From the far end of Cowick Street, at the foot of St John's Cross Hill, they ran practically to Whipton and back and gave plenty of warning of their approach. It is of interest to record that at that time conductors received 14/- per week and drivers 27/6d. To help the circulation of the trams a new bridge was built over the Exe in 1905. I was shown it for the first time, in either 1905 or 1906, on the occasion of the Exeter Carnival of that year. My father stood on the left-hand side facing Fore Street Hill with me perched on his shoulder as the fire-engines and decorated wagons, drawn by huge carthorses in gleaming and colourful harness, passed on their journey up the hill to the High Street and beyond. I remember my father drawing my attention explicitly to the new bridge on which we stood.

Motor cars were first compelled to be registered in 1904: Exeter registrations amounted to twelve in that first year, the registration letters 'FJ' being the initials of Mr F J Widgery, the Mayor at that time. In 1907 the number of registrations had grown to 70, and by 1912 to 225 - so there was no car problem at that time for the pedestrian. The wandering schoolboy would have been more likely to have seen a bolting horse, a runaway bullock or an organ-grinder with his organ and monkey!

There were usually quite large numbers of farm animals being driven, on foot, through the streets of Exeter on Fridays, either on their way to the Bonhay Road Cattle Market or to the slaughterhouses, or back to the farms. I helped my uncle on one such event while staying at his farm in Thorverton. He had a number of bullocks for sale in the Exeter market, seven miles away. We started on the Thursday evening, taking the cattle to a farmyard at Upton Pyne where it had been arranged they should rest for the night. My auntie fetched us back to the farm from the yard and, early next morning, drove us to Upton Pyne to continue the journey. Stick in hand I had to walk in front of the line of bullocks, so preventing their dispersal, while my uncle brought up the rear, keeping them on the move in the right direction. We proceeded thus until we arrived, to my great relief, at the market and the cattle were safely confined to the pen allotted to them. I was well paid for this effort, my uncle slipping me a two-shilling piece when the mission was completed.

One of my fairly regular excursions from Church Road, as a child, was to Ide Brook, armed with jam-pot and fishing net, in search of minnows. The journey was an easy one for me: up Church Road, along the lane behind the grandstand of the County Ground and then diagonally across the sloping fields, and at that time houseless roads, to the foot of Constitution Hill. I knew this as "roly-poly hill", a steep, narrow lane leading to the summit. The view, as one topped the crest and wandered down the grassy path, was indescribably beautiful, it was agricultural Devon at its loveliest - just a farm

here and there, white or pink-washed and thatched. A
narrow, winding road, screened by the many leafy trees,
led from Alphington Church on one's left to the cluster
of houses running up to the Huntsman's Inn on the right.
Beyond, the railed lane ran down to a path across the
wooded meadow and so down to the little winding stream
of the Ide Brook. This was easily accessible and was
normally shallow, so I usually succeeded in catching a
few unfortunate minnows to carry home in triumph.

The business in St Thomas appeared to flourish.
Indeed round about 1907 or 1908, following some illness,
Mother was able to have a week's holiday, taking me with
her. We travelled by train to Sidmouth and thence by
horse-drawn cab to a relative who owned a boarding-house
in the town. I remember only two things about that
holiday: one was this cab-drive with Mother and me
inside the cab and the driver, reins in hand, on his box
seat high above us. The other was the delight given us

by the Pierrot Concerts, which took place on a circular steel staging erected on the beach at the Budleigh Salterton end of the Esplanade, linked to the mainland by a short gangway. The Pierrots, in their traditional white costumes with black spots, performed each afternoon and evening while we were there, and collections were taken from time to time from those who gathered round.

Another trip in one of those early years was to Exmouth (Day Return ticket 1/-), where we boarded the *Duchess of Devonshire* steamer for a trip along the coast

and back one afternoon, followed by tea at Exmouth and then home. I am glad to say Mother had chosen a very fine day for this respite and I certainly thoroughly enjoyed the experience. I think there was only one other trip we made together and that was a ride on the top deck of one of the city's trams from St Thomas to the terminus near Whipton and back on the same tram; at that time that was another new experience for me. My parents, incidentally, were never able, in the whole of their married life, to have a joint holiday.

Retter's Dairy

My father invested in a pony and milk cart, the latter a covered-in creation with its floor only six inches or so from the ground. It was a miniature "Western covered waggon" with its cover painted bright yellow and the words 'C RETTER, Dairyman' boldly printed on the sides. It was the first of its kind in the city and the idea was quickly copied by larger dairy firms. Large milk churns could fairly easily be lifted into this cart: they contained new milk and scald milk. There was no bottle delivery of course - jugs were brought to the float by householders and my father served the milk from the appropriate churn by means of long-handled pint and half-pint measures. New milk, as far as I recall, was sold for about 2d a pint and scald milk for 1d. Scald milk was the residue left after new milk had been slowly heated and the cream, so brought to the surface, removed after cooling. This was the famous "clotted cream" and when unsold it was turned, by hand, into butter.

In Affectionate Remembrance of

" They did their work ; their day is done."

" Ring out the old, ring in the new."

The EXETER HORSE TRAMS

Which succumbed to an Electric Shock, April 4th, 1905.

Butter making was a daily task for most farmers' wives since the weekly sale of this product was, by tacit agreement, part of her private income.

The cream, contained in a large bowl, was stirred by hand - literally - the rotation continuing for at least twenty minutes and sometimes, if it refused to "turn", for as long as an hour, until at last the mixture settled down to a reasonably solid mass of butter surrounded by the buttermilk. The time taken varied with the weather and on sultry days could lead to the intense irritation of the housewife; I took care to keep out of sight and sound when I saw that kind of situation developing!

The butter was thoroughly washed with cold water, salted and then removed from the bowl and shaped with the use of two wooden butter-pats. It was divided into half-pound lumps with the aid of the dairy scales, after which the final shaping of it took place. Sometimes it was sold having been flattened and then rolled up, rather like a short Swiss roll, or alternatively it was worked into a cylindrical shape and a design such as a swan imprinted on the top surface. The wooden pats used frequently had to be dipped into cold, clean water to prevent the butter sticking to them.

In the hands of a skilled operator this process of weighing, shaping, stamping and finally placing on a square of greaseproof paper would be a matter of moments - it was the actual stirring of the cream which took by far the greater time.

My parents also invested in a marvellous rubber-wheeled and elegant governess car with slender, curved shafts: a most beautiful outfit. Pony-drawn, it could carry two people comfortably, one on each of its cushioned sides, and had a small entrance doorway and step at the back. I have seen an almost identical such governess car in the Bristol Museum in recent years.

I recall one journey only in this and that was from a farm at Honiton Clyst home to St Thomas, after midnight, following a Sunday visit. The trap had two side-lamps, candle-powered, and with this illumination my parents drove home. I was placed on the floor, a highly comfortable position, to be lulled by the movement of the trap and with the stars above to wonder at.

Meanwhile, the business had been extended to include a few groceries. Sugar, for example, arrived in one-hundredweight boxes and was weighed out into individual one-pound bags made of stout blue paper: filling and weighing these bags provided one or two of the older children with interest and excitement.

Ice-cream was also sold, it consisting simply of sweet frozen custard. The custard was placed in a metal cylinder about 18 inches long and 10 inches in diameter;

through the centre of the lid of this can there passed a metal rod to the inside end of which was attached a paddle arrangement, while the outer end was attached to a foot-long handle. This contraption was then placed in a larger container and packed round with ice. The conversion to ice-cream was effected by turning the handle and so maintaining the custard in motion within, quite a lengthy process at times.

The ice was obtained in solid blocks measuring some three feet in length and having roughly a one-footsquare cross-section. It usually arrived wrapped in sacking and was deposited in the dairy which had been built at the back of the house. Chopping the necessary amount of ice from this lump, and then breaking it down to fit around the custard container, was another awkward task.

Hard Times in Church Road

By 1911 there were five of us children at Church Road. To help pay the rent my parents let the best first-floor bedroom with its French window and balcony. Their first lodger was a very elderly man known as "Grandfather Turl". He became bedridden and presumably died - I can recall nothing of this. What I do recall is that many years later when my father needed an additional mattress, he took Grandfather Turl's from the cellar and found five golden sovereigns tucked away inside it. There was great jubilation at home that day: the find just covered the quarter's rent.

Grandfather Turl was followed by two elderly ladies, the Misses Mills, the older of these again almost bedridden. I recall one exciting and frightening time when their plaster ceiling collapsed and unpeeled itself, with its heavy load of plaster, from the corner of the room immediately above the elder Miss Mills' bed - it was an extremely lucky escape for her as the peeling from the ceiling did not break but hung in one piece, with the weight taken by the foot of the bed and the floor beside it. The plaster had begun to break away at that stage and the room was covered with dust and small bits. The younger Miss Mills' bed had escaped completely. It was all sorted out somehow but I was too young to be affected by, or perhaps to notice, the subsequent repairs.

Probably both Grandfather Turl and old Miss Mills died on the premises but I knew nothing of either event. There was a young lady, by the name of Lily Hill, who acted as nursemaid at that time and I have no doubt that I was taken for long walks by Lily on any abnormal occasion. Lily was a great favourite. She was the daughter of a Police Sergeant who, in due course, retired and became the licencee of the Exeter Inn (with its skittle alley) at Thorverton. Lily married and herself became the licencee, with her husband, of the Cowley Bridge Inn near Exeter, where I met her as a customer a number of times in the 'twenties. Later, the Searles (Lily and her husband) took over the Turk's Head adjacent to the Guildhall. I think after that they were at an inn in Castle Street. The last time I met Lily was at the Turk's Head - a very large, jolly woman. I have no doubt she will be remembered by many of the older generation of Exonians.

GUILDHALL AND HIGH STREET, EXETER

When we later left Church Road the younger Miss Mills had, of course, to find another home. This proved to be a room in a small tenement house situated in an alley somewhere in the block of houses then standing between the bottom of North Street and the beginning of Bartholomew Street. At Mother's request I visited her there on two or three occasions around the years 1913-15. The room contained a narrow single bed with, on one side, a small wash-stand with bowl and jug and on the other a small table and a couple of chairs. On the table she kept her trinkets, miniatures of Bristol and its Suspension Bridge set in glass paper-weights, and her meagre store of crockery. For heating and cooking she used a little paraffin lamp, with a three-inch wick, protected from draughts by a small frame which supported a trivet capable of carrying a frying-pan or a kettle. Here, in extreme poverty, Miss Mills lived out the last year or two of her life.

In the Heart of Exeter

At the age of six I was admitted to St John's Hospital
School which was run then on a fee-paying basis, these
being 4/- a term for the young pupils, rising to 5/- a
term for the older boys. The school stood on the right-
hand side of the High Street, behind the line of shops,
and was entered through a large gate, some eight to ten
feet wide, which stood at the end of a little arcade of
the same depth as the shops on either side. One passed
through a small gate which formed part of the large gate
into the playground. The main buildings were on the
left, the first entrance on that left-hand side being
for the use of older boys in the class known as X7,
which was at that time (1909) in the charge of Mr
Howells. Mr Howells' class was regarded with awe, for
his pupils were taught woodwork and French. The next
object on the left was a solid stone statue of a "Blue
Coat" boy, set closely within two protecting walls and
abutting on the classroom which projected from the main
building. There was a separate entrance to this classroom, which was in my time occupied by Class 4, the
master there being Mr Bishop.

He arrived new to the school probably in 1910 or 1911.
When my mother heard of his appointment she recalled
that she had known a boy of that name who had been
brought up in the same home area as her own, at
Lympstone; somewhat timidly I mentioned this to the new
master, who remembered my mother and was obviously
delighted to have found some slight link with his child-
hood days. I remember Mr Bishop for his unfailing

kindness and enthusiasm - especially was this latter evident in his singing lessons when, standing on a chair and conducting classes before him, he more than once demolished, with his baton, the electric light and shade hanging near him from the ceiling!

The main building of the school continued beyond and behind Mr Bishop's classroom and was entered through a large Norman-style door at the far end, the whole building consisting simply of a very large and high hall. This hall had in all probability originally housed the whole school. As far as I recall, Classes 1, 2 and 3 were arranged side by side on rising tiers of desks on the right-hand side of the hall and Class X7 was at the far end of these three, separated completely from the lower classes by a wooden screen which reached to the ceiling. The Headmaster's desk stood on a little platform in the left-hand corner of this triple class-room. Adjoining this was a communicating door with X7, while a small cupboardway on the left-hand side of the room, just below the desk, led to Mr Bishop's classroom. Between each of the three classes curtains some six or seven feet high could be drawn to separate them.

For my first year at St John's I sat in this first class under the care of Mr Godfrey - a quiet, unassuming and kindly master. We were at first issued with slates but after a short interval each boy was given a Copy Book, the pages of which were lined and headed by four or five words which were to be copied on the lines below. The principle was that lines drawn upwards were lightly written while downward strokes were made more heavily, both upward and downward strokes being vertical; each line on each page was to be a copy of the top line. This formed our first introduction to the use of pen and ink; we had to supply our own pens and nibs but inkwells were placed in the desks at which we sat. I should add that each of the four or five rising tiers in the separate classrooms took one long desk at which some five or six boys could sit. The work was heavily biased in favour of the "3 Rs" and with these there was emphasis on the learning of tables and mental arith-metic.

18

The right-hand side of the playground was flanked by a
long shed behind which there were additional classrooms.
Entry to these was effected from a small passage which
led from the playground to Bampfylde Street. One of
these classrooms had Mr Orchard as master: rather grim
in appearance, he was at heart a very kindly man, though
the fact was occasionally blurred by the use of a
highly-polished round ruler which was apt to descend
unexpectedly at times across the knuckles of the unwary!
He was also extremely well-read and hardly a day passed
without his bowler-hatted figure being seen searching
through the shelves of Commins' second-hand bookshop in
the High Street.

At the far end of the playground
stood the Headmaster's house and on
its right, apparently part of the
same block, there were two more
classrooms. One - possibly Class 5
- on the upstairs floor was in the
charge of Mr Ponsford, a fine
teacher but inclined to be sarcas-
tic and one who used the cane
(across the hands) when homework
failed to reach the standard expected of us. I remember on one
occasion he caned every boy in turn
for badly-drawn maps, even though
he had given 9 marks out of 10 to
two of his victims: "They should
have got 10!" he said. Four of us held an indignation
meeting in the playground, just outside the door of this
building, after school that day and discussed some form
of reprisal. Unfortunately, after a few minutes Mr
Ponsford came out and with a nasty snarl sent us off at
the double; the rebellion died then.

"Late Again, Retter?"

The Headmaster was Mr Reginald Smith, known always as
"the Boss". I met him "formally", so to speak, on two
occasions. I had been late a number of times and,
exasperated, the class-master sent me to the Head. I

19

went quaking, was told to hold out my right hand and was then given one stroke with the cane across it; I hardly felt the impact and went back to my class almost smiling with relief. Two days later I was late again and was once more sent to "the Boss". This time I was cool and unruffled. Mr Smith grunted "What, you late again?" Once more I put my hand out - but with a vastly different result: this time he put the whole of his weight behind the blow. Wringing my hand and putting it to my lips to ease the sting, I turned to leave but a sharp voice said "Stand still! The other hand please!"; I then received a second crashing whack across the palm of the left hand. I was then sent back to my class with the warning ringing in my ears "Don't let me see you here again!" Needless to say, he didn't.

I remember on one occasion seeing him hurrying, cane in hand, across the hall following an intended victim who was apparently in a very great hurry to get home. Apart from these two or three "local disturbances" the cane was rarely seen and very rarely needed to be used.

Under Mr Smith's guidance and discipline, and with a tremendous emphasis on work given by every member of the staff, the school had gained and held supremacy in the winning of the City Scholarships to Hele's School. It seemed to be the case that of some twenty-four scholarships awarded each year, about twenty would go to pupils of St John's.

Little remains in my memory of actual lessons except the occasional interludes afforded by students from what was then the University College. These came at intervals, armed always with a very large painting or drawing designed to illustrate the particular lesson they were giving. It was at St John's that I first made the acquaintance of such poems as The Deserted Village, The Lady of Shalott and The Wreck of the Hesperus. I remember that in Mr Ponsford's year we had a class "library" formed by the gift of one book from each boy plus a few books from the previous year.

An Exeter Martyr
The last twenty or thirty yards of the playground on

20

the left-hand side were flanked by a wall, beyond which was a strip of garden and beyond that, part of a Roman wall; I recall just one session in that garden. It must have been a very unusual occurrence but while we were engaged in digging, "the Boss" came along and remarked that this was ground which had probably been cultivated by the Romans two thousand years before. I can remember only this one gardening effort: I imagine "rain spoilt play" for all the other lessons that might have been planned under the general heading of Nature Study.

What "the Boss" did not tell us on that occasion was that Agnes Prest, a Protestant, had been martyred at a spot at the top of Southernhay which could only have been some hundred yards distant from the wall at that point. She was burnt at the stake, after a period of imprisonment in the Castle, for refusing to change her religious beliefs during the reign of Philip and Mary, the date being 15 August 1557. It is quite extraordinary that, living in Southernhay for so many years, I remained unaware of this barbaric episode until recently.

My journeys to and from the school were events in themselves. After becoming familiar with the High Street, Fore Street, Bridge Street, Exe Bridge and Cowick Street line of travel, I gradually varied the exercise by using the many fascinating parallel side-roads - such as down Stepcote Hill and past St Mary Steps Church - all leading finally to Exe Bridge. There

was a tram service from St Thomas' which passed the school but on no occasion did I ever make use of it.

On one memorable day - it must have been in 1909 - my father met me and placed me in the large basket he carried on the front of his bicycle, with my feet dangling over the front, and gave me a lift home. I recall clearly his remarks on the care needed to avoid the tramlines: "If I get my front wheel in one of those we'll come off with a bump," he said.

Occasionally I took sandwiches to school for lunch or alternatively was given 3d which enabled me to purchase a cup of tea (price 1d) and two large currant buns in Depaoli's Restaurant, just below the school. In 1913 this little cafe was transferred to premises a few steps along Castle Street on its right-hand side.

Fridays formed, for me, the peak of each week: arithmetic and dictation tests in the morning - these were of course marked immediately - while the afternoon consisted, for the most part, of silent reading during which the master was enabled to complete his register or any other clerical task demanded of him.

The dinner break, 12.00 to 2.00, had its excitement too, since on that day my journey home to St Thomas invariably took me through the lower market. This stood, as old Exonians well know, at the top of Fore Street, on the left-hand side.

Wandering around amongst its many stalls I was pretty certain to meet one or other of my farming relations. If this comb failed - and still on my way home - I would wander round the cattle market in Bonhay Road. There were always large numbers of farmers here watching and listening to the auctioneers describing the good points of the animals, penned before them, and then opening the bidding for the lots they had to offer. I recall in particular Uncle Aaron of Holbrook Farm at Honiton Clyst, who never failed to produce a copper or two when we met. There was one occasion, though, when after the usual courtesies, "How's Auntie?", "How's your Mother?" and so on, we stood looking at one another in silence for a full minute. Now a minute in a child's life, like the politician's week, is a very long time but at last

23

Uncle's brow cleared, the slightly puzzled look disappeared and he said "Oh, of course" and put his hand into his trouser pocket to find the usual 2d. A relieved "Thank you!" and a quick wave and we went our separate ways. A gift of this magnitude made the week for me.

Exeter Floods

There was one week, in 1910, when it is pretty certain no market could have been held. After heavy rain the Exe overflowed its banks and St Thomas was flooded to such an extent that boats had to be used to ferry people to and from their houses. In a volume of newspaper cuttings collected by the then Town Clerk, Mr H Lloyd Parry, appears a cartoon taken from the *Flying Post* showing Cowick Street deep in flood water with a woman struggling and crying "Help! Help!" Floating near her are two gramophones of the time; from the horn of one, labelled 'The Town Clerk's Office', comes the remark "Sympathy but no remedy", while from the other, labelled 'The Surveyor's Office', comes "No records of any floods". The caption reads:

Cowick Street Woman: "Help! Help!"
Municipal Chorus: "Don't bother us now - besides we're trying to buy some baths so that you can learn to swim."

Strangely enough I can personally recall nothing of these floods. They must, I think, have coincided with an attack of measles which I had and which would have kept me in bed for a week or two.

Friends and Foes

The period 1912-13 was a lean one for the Church Road family. Pocket money was unheard of and if the Friday "uncle hunt" proved fruitless I was thrown back on the hope of being allowed to share in a more wealthy friend's purchase. This particular friend was George Parish, whose father was a policeman with an enviable wage rising from 22/6d at the start to 30/- per week after ten years and George could rely on a steady ha'penny a week; at that time this would purchase two strips of liquorice or a sizeable bag of sweets.

As well as my friend George Parish, I remember a few of the names of other boys who were in my class at St John's. One was a lad named Paul, a very delicate boy who walked with a pronounced stoop and who died around about 1911. Then there was Pentecost, another friend who lived in the St Thomas area and who was afflicted with a perpetual cold. Two brothers named Langmead, probably twins, terrified me for a few days by announcing solemnly that they had formed a gang and were going to "do" any boy they met after school on the way home. I recall that for a short time I pursued some very devious paths to Exe Bridge but nothing happened and the threats soon ceased to worry me.

Then there was one, Jimmy James, who explained to me after school one day exactly where babies came from. I remember the widening grin on his silly face when he perceived my complete disbelief and disgust. I hurried home that day and told my mother the horrid news. She

25

said, "He's a very naughty boy to tell you a thing like that. When your father comes home I'll send him round to Mrs James to tell her the stories her Jimmy has been telling you. I'm sure he'll get a thrashing from his mother." With that reply I was completely reassured and delighted to think that Jimmy would get the thrashing he deserved. The whole subject then and there passed from my mind and I do not recall ever speaking again to Jimmy.

The County Ground

1911 was an outstanding year, marking the Coronation of King George V and Queen Mary.

There were three memorable events during that summer. One was the Mass Drill of the Exeter Schools, carried out one afternoon at the County Ground, St Thomas. For this event one group of schools turned out wearing red jerseys, another white and the third, which included St John's, blue. I remember we had a number of rehearsals marching around the playground in twos and fours and learning to keep in step. On the day in question the "blue" schools met at St John's and then, preceded by the band of the Fourth Battalion Devon Regiment and Exonia Military Band, marched in columns of four to the County Ground. Three thousand children took part in this Empire Pageant. Of course it rained steadily at first so that by the time we reached St Thomas we were all thoroughly soaked. The rain did stop a little later and then under Mr W G Hodge the red, white and blue masses marched, forming intricate patterns on the green-sward. I was told later that it had been a highly successful pageant and this is confirmed in an extract from the *Evening Post* of 24 June 1911 which refers to the "unique contribution" of the city's schools to the Coronation celebrations.

The second event in that year was the "Coronation Tea". For this, two long rows of trestle tables with forms on each side were set up in the long shed in the playground. The boys sat at these tables and each found in front of him a Coronation mug and a paper bag with sandwiches, cakes and so on. The mugs were duly filled

with tea and then became the property of each individual. I have no doubt that at least some of the mugs
presented to us on that day are still in existence and
perhaps now form prized heirlooms. The third event was
a "Grand Firework Display", again at the County Ground
and probably on the evening of the Pageant. I have only
a hazy idea of this but I believe it terminated a little
earlier than expected when a falling blazing star landed
in a very large box of fireworks!

SUMMER TERM - Additional Arithmetic
The year 1913 was the pre-scholarship year for the
class I was in. There were two examinations to be faced
by would-be Heleans. The first, in arithmetic and
English, was taken by all. For the successful few who
reached a qualifying standard there was a second examination, at a later date, in history and geography,
together with an interview. In retrospect it seemed to
me that at St John's the greater part of our time went
to arithmetic, my impression being that the scripture
lessons were quietly dropped. There was homework of
about an hour's duration, set twice weekly, earmarked
for history and geography. I think "Gill's Geography"
was the foundation book we used for that subject and we
had to learn long lists of capes, headlands, rivers and
towns of the British Isles. I was no artist and my
efforts to produce pleasing and accurate maps rarely won
more than a snort of contempt.
    In the summer term additional instruction in arith-
metic could be obtained from the Headmaster who ran an
early-morning class at the school between 7.00 and 7.45
a.m. each day, the fee being 6d per week. I found this,
strangely enough, interesting, useful and even enjoy-
able: arithmetic was my favourite subject and the early
morning call presented no difficulties. I do not know
how Mother found the necessary 6d each week but the fact
remains that she did and it was much to my advantage.
Wealthier pupils, incidentally, could learn swimming at
the Exeter Baths in school time, also at 6d per lesson,
but the line for me was drawn necessarily at the early
morning arithmetic.

- Extra Excursions!

For me that last summer term at St John's was a pleasant one for a reason readily appreciated: this was that the school had a complete holiday on each of four successive Wednesdays in June and July. So many Sunday School outings were arranged in Exeter each summer that school work had been seriously interrupted, complaints grew and finally the churches agreed to arrange their outings on one or other of these four Wednesdays. Presumably the school term was appropriately lengthened but I remember even now how pleasant were those mid-week breaks.

I took part in one such outing with St Thomas' Church; we were taken by train to Dawlish in the morning and given tea in a hall beside Dawlish Water. Another outing I remember in about 1910 or 1911 was organised by the Primrose League, a junior branch of the Conservative Party. Starting from the little hall on the left-hand side of Cowick Street, between Exe Bridge and St Thomas Station, we were taken in two very large four-wheeled wagonettes called "brakes", each with two long benches fitted parallel to the wheels and drawn by two or four horses, to Mamhead Park where we were entertained to tea by Sir Robert Newman. He subsequently became Member of Parliament for Exeter and, at a later date, Lord Mamhead. We returned to Exeter in the course of the evening to the strains of "For He's a Jolly Good Fellow" and "We All Go the Same Way Home".

Those early years at St John's were happy ones.

Country Ways and Holidays

While we were still living in Church Road I remember
being sent sometimes to stay with an aunt at Ashley Farm
near Thorverton. On most Fridays this aunt - one of my
mother's sisters - came to Exeter on business, stabling
her pony and trap at the Moreton Inn which then existed
on the right-hand side of Cowick Street opposite and
just beyond St Thomas Station. The stabling
accommodation lay behind the inn and was reached by
driving, with head ducked, through a low covered passage
between the inn and the next dwelling house. Once in
the yard, the ostler took over, enquiring only at what
time in the afternoon the outfit would be required
again. So it was to the Moreton Inn that I repaired
when visiting Thorverton.

On rare occasions Uncle would accompany her and my
journey to the farm would take place seated on the
narrow back portion of the two front seats. Here,
clinging grimly to the vertical back of the driver's
seat, I faced the road behind me. The drive was never
without its hazards even, for example, on the short haul
from the inn over Exe Bridge to Bonhay Road - there
seemed always a tram to be passed, a fearful experience
for the pony and a nerve-racking one for me.

Two places on this adventurous drive stand out. One
was a spot where, I was told, the pony had once bolted,
the trap had overturned and Auntie had been thrown out,
luckily unharmed. The other was the Hangman's Tree, a
mile or two down the road towards Thorverton, with its
long horizontal branch from which, in the past, the

29

bodies of bandits had been hung in chains as a grim warning to other would-be highwaymen.

We obtained our first view of the farm from the top of Perry Hill. Beneath us lay the cluster of thatched barns and farmhouses, with the road to Cadbury running alongside it. On the other side of this lane, throwing their shadows over the farm, stood three magnificent beech trees. Beyond the beech trees a meadow, Roosing Ham, fell steeply away to a primrose-edged stream in the valley below which wound its way through the narrow copse and meadows of Dashelly Ham and Rye Arrish to the village and so to the Exe. To the right, Home Cleave and Cleave Orchard gave way to the fields rising away to the manor of the Fursdons in the distance.

On arrival at the farm after this drive from Exeter, Uncle would go immediately to the wood-rick at the back of the house, place a whole huge bundle in the fireplace and set the fire going. While Auntie prepared tea, Uncle went back to tend the pony and I sat absorbing the wonderful smell of burning wood, while enjoying the welcome heat.

The farmhouse must have been over three hundred years old and was built of cob and thatch. There is a saying that all cob needs are "strong shoes and a good hat", meaning a firm base and a well-constructed thatched roof. This house, in its old age, needed further support. This was given by a solid metal bar running the length of the house just above the bedroom ceilings, to the exterior ends of which were attached two large iron crossbars, shaped like huge multiplication signs, clasping the ends of the house in their embrace.

The courtyard was the end point of many a pig's journey through life. I remember one such occasion when a huge elliptic wooden tub, about eight or nine feet by five feet and some twelve inches deep, was placed there. Uncle disappeared into the orchard from which, a few minutes later, the most appalling shrieks and squeals arose, Uncle reappearing with the pig to be slaughtered. I cannot describe adequately the terror of that animal - it was as if it had known itself to be doomed the moment

Uncle's hand seized it in that sunlit orchard.   The end was, however, speedy.

   After the first night away from home, these holidays gave me great happiness.   In those days, before the First World War, many more men were employed on such small farms than is the case today.   I was able to enjoy the delights of hay-making, harvesting, threshing and cider-making in their seasons.
   There were always, too, the pleasures of a noisy airgun (without ammunition) and a wonderful miniature four-wheeled trolley with its seat just large enough for a six-year-old.   Seated in this conveyance on the gently sloping road outside the yard and with the steering-rod handle firmly held I could get a clear run of perhaps ten yards, after which the thing would come to a halt and it would be necessary to alight and push the trolley back to its starting point again. I was content to perform this operation a dozen or more times in succession, the repetition being part of the fun.

   On rare oc-

casions I was permitted to assist Auntie with the afternoon milking. Equipped with bucket and three-legged
stool, I was shown how the process was carried out and
somewhat timidly I would set to work. No doubt to its
relief, my cow was dealt with finally by Auntie herself.

I learnt also the extraordinary command of abuse which
some of the labourers enjoyed. As a matter of course at
the end of a day's work the heavy carthorses standing in
the yard would have their shoes examined for any embed-
ded stones. Holding the upturned foot of a massive
giant of a horse balanced on its three remaining legs
was no light task by any standard and the consequent
flow of adjectives addressed to "Bessie" or "Violet" was
something that enlarged enormously the scope of a
child's vocabulary. I did not personally meet again
such powers of descriptive analysis until I joined the
Scouts and discovered that English working boys gleaned
more than just technical skills at their places of
employment!

I rarely went out at night but there was one time on a
summer visit when I was taken by Uncle after dark to
assist in dealing with a wasp nest which had been
singled out for destruction. Armed with syringe and
hurricane lamp, he led me in the silent darkness through
a couple of fields until we reached the nest. While I
held the lamp Uncle quietly injected into the mouth of
the nest the contents of the syringe. The next day I
was told the wasps were "done for".

Among the most outstanding events for me in those
early years at Ashley were the harvest teas. At the
farm Auntie would prepare a number of cheese, ham, honey
and jam sandwiches, filling a large wicker basket with
these together with a couple of dozen small home-made
cakes. She made about two gallons of strong tea, plus
home-made lemonade for the children, and at about 4.30
p.m. one of the helpers from the field would return to
the farm to assist with the transport out to the
harvesting. There were usually about half a dozen

labourers to be provided for. Some of the men had their own cider supply but most of the company preferred a drink of tea at that time. It was a short break as far as the men were concerned but the rest of us prolonged the picnic at the side of the field, keeping a watchful eye on our ever-hungry dog.

The Thorverton area was quite hilly and the fields were relatively small so it was easy for rabbits to escape into the hedges as the corn was cut, but I remember certain harvest days on flatter ground towards Honiton where the fields were many times larger. Cutting would proceed for many hours and the rabbits were confined in a smaller and smaller space, being afraid to make the long run to the nearest hedge. In due course, the farmer and his neighbours arrived with guns, took station around the diminishing corn and the last few rounds of the harvester would be accompanied by the sound of shots and warning shouts. The shouting was essential at times, since the cartridges used for this purpose were filled with hundreds of small lead shot which spread in the course of projection; I remember my father showing me a couple of black marks on his right arm which revealed the presence of shot which had caught him unawares on one of these "shoots".

There were usually sufficient rabbits available so that anyone around the field could be given one. The farmers took the remainder as a small supplement to their income - rabbits sold at 4d or 6d each in the market.

A few weeks after the harvest came the cider-making. At Ashley I remember the cider cellar contained some twenty barrels, or hogsheads as they were called, in two rows arranged so that they lay on a framework which kept them off the ground, flat ends vertical and facing a gravel path which ran from one end of the cellar to the other.

The flavour and the strength of the cider depended of course on the period allowed for fermentation and also on the previous contents of the hogsheads. I remember once a remarkably happy blend being obtained from the cider stored in what had been a rum cask; I have also heard and read of various additions such as a lump of cheese being added by farmers to give a distinctive flavour to a particular cask.

Enough cider was made to supply the farm labourers with their gallon-a-day firkinful ration throughout the year.

My aunt told me that one day one of her geese had wandered into the barn when the cider making was in progress and had found the yield very much to her liking. Apparently it had imbibed steadily at intervals throughout the day, being found finally stone dead in a corner of the barn. It was taken to the farmhouse and my aunt promptly stripped it of its feathers in the utility room to be prepared next morning for the market.

However, at first light there arose a tremendous cackling and squawking from this room and the so-called "dead" bird was found fluttering in anxious and indignant desperation in the midst of the pile of her own feathers. Auntie had to make a pair of very short trousers and a suitable waistcoat, buttoning along the back, to preserve its body heat and to enable it to return - a fearful and warning sight no doubt - to its farmyard companions! That was her story!!

In one of those early years the usual visit to Ashley was Auntie Sally, one of my father's sisters. I travelled by train to Teignmouth, where I was met by Auntie with

her two daughters. We walked the length of the
Teignmouth sea-front and then crossed by ferry (one
penny for adults, half fare for children) to Shaldon. A
long walk followed through the village to the hamlet of
Ringmore, with the Teign on our right. We turned left,
climbed a country lane and arrived at what was then a
modern brick-built four-bedroomed house set a few yards
off the road.

To its left stood a small, two-storied barn. I
discovered that the house had been let to summer-holiday
visitors. The four of us slept on the upper floor of
the barn, reached by climbing vertically a number of
wooden rungs fixed to the lower part of the barn. Here,
four separate beds were made up a few feet apart and
each night closed with the prayers "Lighten our Darkness" and the Lord's Prayer. It was the first occasion
on which I had heard family prayers and felt the deep
sense of peace and security which they brought.

Of that week I have only this memory and that of the
ferry crossing.

Gentlemen's " Roscut,"
from **55/-**

Ladies' " Roscut,"
from **50/-**

Surviving in St Thomas

Among the older citizens of Exeter, in the years 1910 and 1911, there was great excitement regarding the swaying fortunes of the Liberal and Unionist Parties. Following the city's representation by a Liberal MP from 1906-1910, the Conservative Unionist candidate, Mr Henry Duke, was elected early in 1910 with a majority of 26. In a second election held later in the same year the Liberal candidate, Mr Richard Harold St Maur, was elected with a majority of 4. The Conservatives petitioned for a re-count - which was granted - and in April 1911 Mr Duke was elected with a majority of one! These events had little impact on nine- and ten-year-olds but I remember the large number of yellow and blue rosettes which were sported by children at that time.

From about this date the business in Church Road began to run down. Mother's health deteriorated and she began to suffer from bronchitis and asthma. The doctor's visits became more frequent and, to crown misfortune, the pony, finding the corn-bin open one day, proceeded to gorge himself and died within hours. In some way a replacement pony also succumbed.

Further, during one of Mother's illnesses my father invested some £200, which he had just received from his father's estate, in the purchase of three small houses; as income became insufficient to meet bills, Father found, when forced to re-sell the houses, that he could do so only at a substantial loss. Creditors became more pressing and in October 1912 he had to admit defeat and declare himself bankrupt. I remember my mother in tears in the little room behind the shop, surrounded by a mass of bills, receipts, counterfoils and legal documents.

The business had to be sold. Nothing had been placed in my mother's name and we were left with only the bare necessities of life. We had to leave Church Road, of course, and - ironically - rent at £12 per year one of the very houses which my father had owned but a short time before.

My father had a number of brothers, either farming or in business, and they succeeded in persuading him that to live down the disgrace of bankruptcy his best plan was to emigrate. Accordingly, in late 1912, he booked a passage to Toronto, hoping to establish, in due course, a home for his family.

With some bitterness my mother recounted later that his relatives had given him £20 but, to prevent any of this being slipped to Mother, it was not handed to him until he was in the train and about to leave Exeter.

We were thus left in Oakfield Road, St Thomas, quite penniless and with Mother in poor health. Although I did not realise it at the time, Mother was pregnant, my brother Roy being born in December of that year. My sister, then about twelve years of age, was taken from school and became in effect a second mother in the house.

The lower front room (for which there was no furniture anyway) was used as a shop and some grocery goods left from the Church Road business were displayed on homemade shelves; the front door was propped open and "business" began again.

I just do not remember how, as a family, we survived; undoubtedly we must have received help from a number of sources. I remember the great kindness of Mrs Jarrett who lived in the next house. Her husband was a blind piano-tuner: he could be seen any morning starting off on his rounds with his little black bag and escorted by his young son. Mrs Jarrett, whenever she cooked, seemed to find something which could be spared and passed over the wall to the Retters. There was also Mr Cox, the baker at Ide. He supplied us with stale bread at half price; this was a tremendous help for which we were all most grateful.

Our general expenses were, of course, minimal. Luckily a street gas-lamp existed just outside the house and this provided light for the front of the house. That illumination was switched on manually by a Council employee armed with a long pole with a hook at the end; at dusk he walked round the local roads pulling switches down and in the mornings he reversed the procedures. Electricity was not generally available in small houses; there were gas terminals in most rooms and of course a gas stove in the kitchen. The kitchen lighting proceeded from a "Veritas" gas mantle, which emitted an excellent white light for that one room. As at Church Road, there was of course no bathroom, the bedrooms being supplied only with a wash-basin and jug of water, replenished daily. Each of the bedrooms was also equipped with a chamber pot, stowed under the bed.

As far as clothes were concerned, I remember wearing at this time "knickerbocker" trousers supported by braces and buttoning below the knee; long stockings were worn up to the knees and then turned down to cover the buttons. Shirts and collars were separate articles; for older boys, washable celluloid collars were worn, attached to the back of the shirt by a large stud. The tie would be placed within the celluloid curve and knotted to cover the front stud. On occasion, if necessity demanded it, a celluloid "front" or "dickey" could be worn beneath one's waistcoat to hide a grubby shirt. These collars and fronts could be washed and dried within moments.

Shoes were practically unknown: we wore stout boots, usually hob-nailed or studded with what were known as "blakeys". These latter could be purchased separately but had to be affixed early in the life of the boots or the nails, by which they were attached, would penetrate to the feet. The boots were lace-ups but the tops of the boots usually bore two or three small metal hooks around which the laces were crossed. Leggings could be purchased for boys of twelve to sixteen but I remember owning only one such pair.

For cleaning purposes we used "blacking", a three-inch slice of which would be placed in a saucer and moistened with a wet brush; this mixture was rubbed well into the leather and being slightly oily it helped to keep the boots waterproof. When dry, a very dim shine could be obtained but only with a considerable expenditure of elbow grease; there was nothing equivalent to the modern shoe polishes.

Boots were, in fact, our greatest problem; there were times indeed when only a cardboard sole lay between foot and ground. I still remember the look of despair which settled on Mr Honeywell's face when requested to repair such shoes. Mr Honeywell was the local cobbler, his shop being in Magdalen Street, immediately opposite the

house that we later occupied. He lived on the premises
with his family and passersby could see him working
almost continuously in his shop. His son Leonard joined
him after leaving school and many years later took over
the business, though his father continued to work well
into his eighties. He was, indeed, over ninety when he
died. The whole of that side of Magdalen Street was
demolished many years after the war and Leonard transferred his business to premises on the other side of the
road.

Christmas in Oakfield Road

When Christmas Eve came in 1912 Mother found, somehow,
a two-shilling piece and handing it to my older sister,
Evelyn, she sent the two of us into the city to buy the
Christmas presents for the family. We achieved this
with no difficulty: half-a-dozen oranges at a ha'penny
each for the toes of the stockings and a pennyworth of
beech nuts and the same of chocolate drops. Games of
"ludo" and "snakes and ladders" with cardboard counters
and tiny dice, in containers of matchbox size, cost 1d
each. Then there were rulers, india rubbers, little
notebooks and fairytale books at a ha'penny or a penny
each and a small Christmas stocking (from Japan perhaps)
containing a tiny pair of tin scales and a little tin
oven with tin spoons, frying pan and a lot of coloured
cardboard. This stocking was the least successful
purchase: it gave joy to my youngest sister, then two
years old, as she opened it but we had to throw away the
tin toys immediately - the edges were almost razor-sharp
and could have been lethal. Luckily there were a few
cachous amongst the cardboard and those compensated a
little for the removal of the toys. Most of these items
were purchased at the Penny Bazaar in the centre of the
city; there was no Woolworths at that time.

We reserved one of the two shillings given us for the
purchase of a Christmas cake. This was some six or
seven inches in diameter and about two inches deep, iced
and with the words "Happy Christmas" in red icing
written across the top. It was, of course, wrapped
round with a red band and a small cardboard box provided

for its safe transport.

We certainly enjoyed that Christmas morning - there was no consciousness of poverty or shortage among us. The morning was further cheered by the arrival of a chicken which had apparently been promised to Mother by an Uncle Henry who was a poulterer in Heavitree. The previous year we had had a turkey which my father had won in a raffle.

St Thomas Easter Fair

Easter was marked by the arrival at St Thomas of the annual Easter Fair, the fair field being close to Oakfield Road with an opening leading to Buller Road and another leading to Okehampton Street. The fair wagons, mostly belonging to Hancocks, were drawn by steam engines gleaming with shining brass; we spent hours watching the arrival of these colourful giants of the road. I remember a terrific argument developing on Easter Sunday, at the edge of the field, between one of the fair owners and a number of very irate local inhabitants who objected to such turmoil and work taking place on such a day. The showmen had a bad time that year: with persistent rain and the field rapidly becoming a sea of mud, attendance was extremely poor.

Occasionally, of course, my father sent a little money home but he was living through a Canadian winter. He could find work only as a grocer's assistant and whenever possible he put a few shillings aside to pay for his return ticket to England.

These events were reflected in my personal estate. My mother was unable to pay the five shillings a term fee for my education at St John's and so received a polite letter from the Education Authority suggesting that it might be wiser for her to place me in a Church School, where no fees were payable. With circumstances as they were, Mother had no option but to agree; it must have been a bitter blow for her as she was fully aware of the fine reputation which St John's School rightly enjoyed.

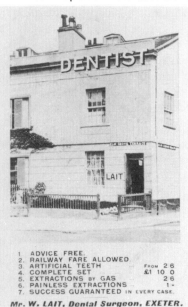

1. ADVICE FREE.
2. RAILWAY FARE ALLOWED
3. ARTIFICIAL TEETH   FROM 2 6
4. COMPLETE SET   £1 10 0
5. EXTRACTIONS BY GAS   2 6
6. PAINLESS EXTRACTIONS   1 -
7. SUCCESS GUARANTEED IN EVERY CASE.

Mr. W. LAIT, Dental Surgeon, EXETER.

As for me, I was very little disturbed; just at that time I was plagued by a succession of raging toothaches and gumboils, so that my face was rarely of normal shape. One just had to put up with this type of trouble until it went. At that time there were no regular school medical inspections; between 1909 and 1921 I recall only one and this must have been at St John's in about 1910 when a lot of us youngsters had chests, ears and eyes tested, our parents being present. Dentists were unknown to us; in fact it wasn't until I was nearly eighteen that I first visited one, being immediately relieved of six teeth.

Just before I left St John's, in the late spring of 1913, my father walked in. We had not been told of his impending arrival: the loss of the *Titanic* was then very much in people's minds, so Mother had witheld the news of his Atlantic crossing until it was safely over.

42

Magdalen St Memories

It now became clear that the Oakfield Road house was too small for us and my parents began to search for larger premises. Their choice fell on 52 East Southernhay, a shop on the bend of the road swinging from Southernhay into Magdalen Street. The house contained six rooms, two on each of three floors, and a flat roof with a summer-house. There was also a kitchen at the back of the shop and fairly extensive cellars. These cellars lay not only beneath the house but had also been excavated beneath the road; they made us wonder whether in its early life the house had been a small inn. There was no back yard and no garden but it did have a number of advantages which I have never experienced since - a butcher's shop fifty yards away; two greengrocers, a dairy and the cobbler's shop opposite; a fish-and-chip shop (chips 1d, fish 2d) within a hundred yards; together with two inns, the "Acorn" and the "Valiant Soldier", in the same road and the letter-box immediately outside the house.

One could get quite a good drink of whisky for 6d - in fact I remember an uncle complaining bitterly, just after one Budget Day, that a bottle of whisky was now costing him 7/6d (37.5 new pence)!

The "Valiant Soldier" at the corner of Magdalen Street and Holloway Street was built, like our house No 52, early in the 18th century as one of the replacements for the houses demolished in the Civil War and was so named to commemorate the brave men who had died during those troubled years. The demolition had been ordered by the

43

defenders when, in 1645, they feared that Fairfax might attack the city from the Topsham side.

Almost within hours of taking up residence in the new house we discovered its main drawbacks: these were quite simply fleas and bugs. It was with horror that we discovered the state, in particular, of the top-most rooms. They were scrubbed with disinfectant, every cupboard was turned out and scoured to the bare boards, tins of "Keatings Powder" were used on the floors and in the crevices, but with only limited success. Finally every scrap of wall-paper was torn down, the windows sealed, sulphur candles lit and the doors and key-holes sealed upon them. After two days the rooms were opened up and scrubbing took place all over again, then they were re-papered and the ceilings whitewashed: the infestation had at last been cleared. The other rooms, below this top floor, were found to be reasonably clean and Mother experienced no difficulty except for the constant hunt after a marauding flea.

No sooner was the bug battle won than the silence of

one of those early nights was broken by the scratching and gnawing of tiny teeth behind the wainscot of my parents' bedroom on the first floor. It was much too loud to have been made by a mouse - indeed it could be heard by those of us who slept in the room above. I may say we were thoroughly frightened and next day emergency methods were adopted to meet this new invader. My father set a spring-steel trap, well baited, in one of the cellars from whence he had proved to himself that the rat - for such it was - had climbed. It was caught and disposed of within a few days and a cat was imported into the household.

The Eye Infirmary

That family cat needed all its nine lives to survive. It seemed to enjoy warm living quarters and frequently took a nap in the rarely-used oven of the kitchen range. One evening someone inadvertently shut the oven door and it was sheer luck for the cat that some time later I released it. I have never seen a cat move so fast in my life as that one did as it made its lightning exit into the cool depths of the cellar. It mercifully survived and was little the worse for its experience though it was never again seen near the oven. With the advent of the cat we had no trouble whatever with mice but a constant war had to be maintained against rats throughout the years that we occupied the house. These animals clearly had a world of their own under the range of two hundred year old houses. There were unfortunately no public rodent operators at that time.

The shop certainly had potential. It was only a short distance from the Devon and Exeter Hospital and the Eye Infirmary, while there was a fairly constant stream of officials to and from the offices into which some of the private houses in Southernhay had been converted, the Rates Office and the Education Office being amongst them.

There were two windows in the shop, one some five feet by two feet and the other two foot six square, with the door between them. The difficulty experienced here was of course the complete lack of capital: hence the smaller window was filled with advertising material from the tobacco companies, while in the larger window rested a huge and slightly battered china swan, forever swimming on a sea of red crepe paper.

A little income was obtained by letting one of the bedrooms and thus a small supply of cigarettes was obtained from a local wholesaler in Holloway Street. We used to buy half a box of "Woodbines" and a few of the standard packets of ten and twenty cigarettes made by Players and Gold Flake; the "Woodbines" retailed at 2d per packet of five or 4d for ten, while the Gold Flake and Players were sold at 6d for ten, 1/- for twenty. The "Woodbines" sold fairly rapidly, netting a profit of between 6d and 1/- and one of us children had then to make a quick dash to the wholesaler for the other half box.

Bed and Breakfast

The first lodger we had was Miss Burnett, an alcoholic, who paid her rent regularly. She left the house about twice a week, clad in an old brown coat and small fur hat, to visit Lawleys the wine merchants in South Street, returning in due course with her renewed supply of whisky. She was evidently determined to drink herself to death and this she did in due course, my parents tending her through her last illness. Her wealthy relatives apparently dealt with the final expenses and funeral arrangements.

Another character who helped to keep rent and rates under control was Mr Maxwell. He was a bed-and-breakfast lodger, disappearing each day and returning, unsteadily, each night after 10 p.m. Our normal bedtime was between 9.00 and 9.30 but we would all be awake in our respective rooms waiting anxiously for his successful negotiation of the bend in the stairs which led to his room. Only once did he fail in this task: on that occasion he slipped down the last four stairs, putting his head through a small glass fanlight.

My father walked him up to the Casualty Department at the hospital, a few painful stitches and a more sober and sorry Mr Maxwell returned to roost. He departed from No 52 in due course to marry the barmaid at his favourite "local" but the double bliss of matrimony and unlimited beer proved too much for him and we heard that he did not survive for long.

There were also occasional visitors for a couple of nights' bed and breakfast. Chief among these were a bookmaker and his wife. He was a big, jolly man clad always in the loudest of check suits and somehow bringing with him a blackboard and easel. They were on their way to the races at Newton Abbot or Haldon. This was before the day of the car, so the following morning they were away long before the normal breakfast time: I suspect they completed most of those journeys on foot. The evenings of their arrival were full of noise and mirth.

Hold-ups to Honiton Clyst

From time to time my father would get a day's work on one of his brothers' farms at Honiton Clyst. This meant a five-mile walk there and back but he would return with a couple of rabbits and a few shillings to the good. He always referred to visits such as these as "going home", for it was at Marlborough, which his brother John farmed, that he had been born. I accompanied him on one such trip. I remember that about a mile and a half from Exeter we went down a slight hill some quarter of a mile in length, flanked on the left-hand side by a thick belt of trees, many of which overhung the road. This, he explained, his voice dropping a little, was known as "Highwaymen's Wood". In his boyhood it was a notoriously unsafe stretch of road: from the darkness of the wood a couple of masked figures could dash out, assault and rob the traveller and disappear in a few seconds back into the gloom. Even horsemen and coaches had been brought to a halt and robbed. For many years I was distinctly nervous of that part of the road to Honiton Clyst. At the present time the last half-mile of this stretch from Exeter has become a maze of motorway constructions and not a tree remains of the highwaymen's haunt; the county misses the ancient ruling of the Church Commissioners that on their lands for every tree cut down, two saplings must be shown to have been planted as successors.

On our walk to Marlborough, as we passed through the village of Honiton Clyst and climbed the hill to the farm, my father told me of the time, somewhere around 1890, when the whole countryside was under snow. Looking out from the farm the roads, hedges and fields had disappeared: there was just one huge, white blanket of snow over everything, only the taller trees projecting, gaunt and leafless, from their white bed. It was during that prolonged and extraordinary snowfall that a train was completely lost for a time on Dartmoor; it was some days, apparently, before the line could be cleared and the passengers and crew rescued. It was during that year, too, I believe, that there was skating on the river at Exeter.

The Exe Valley Railway
There were still, too, occasional visits for me to Ashley. These meant catching the 7.15 a.m. Exe Valley train from St David's Station: a most beautiful journey

EXE VALLEY BRANCH RAILWAY

Narrow Gauge

Up Trains   EXETER TO DULVERTON

Miles from Exeter	STATIONS		WEEK DAYS ONLY					
			A.M.	A.M.	A.M.	P.M.	P.M.	P.M.
	Exeter .. .. dep	7.15	9.45	10.55	1.05	3.05	6.29
3½	Stoke Canon Junction .. .. dep	7.23	9.51	11.03	1.13	3.13	6.36
4½	Brampford Speke .. .. .. arr	7.26	9.54	11.06	1.16	3.17	6.38
6½	Thorverton .. .. arr	7.32	10.00	11.12	1.22	3.24	6.43
7	Up Exe and Silverton .. .. arr	7.38	10.04	11.16	1.26	3.28	6.46
10¼	Cadeleigh and Bickleigh .. .. arr	7.47	10.12	11.24	1.34	3.36	6.54
14¼	Tiverton .. .. arr	7.59	10.23	11.35	1.45	3.48	7.04
21¼	Bampton (Devon) .. .. .. arr	8.18	–	11.51	2.01	4.05	7.20
22¾	Morebath Junction .. .. .. dep	8.27	–	12.00	2.10	4.15	7.29
24¼	Dulverton .. .. arr	8.33	–	12.05	2.15	4.20	7.35

this (9d return) via Stoke Canon and Brampford Speke to Thorverton. The walk of about a mile and a half from the village to the farm was one that I still remember with delight, a delight that increases as the years pass. In spring there were primroses in abundance, followed in later months by cuckoo flowers, dog roses, honeysuckle, an occasional foxglove and a wide variety of other wild flowers whose names I have long since forgotten. The trimming of hedges and verges was in those days the responsibility of the farmer: it was a winter task and was achieved by the use of pruning hooks which left the plant roots unscathed. The devastating effects of weedkillers were happily then unknown.

My walk from the station was always followed by a fried breakfast and a day's freedom to wander among fields and lanes at will, subject only to the lunch call and tea.

Before I left to catch the evening train back, Auntie would bring out a large basket in which she had packed such farm produce as a chicken, butter, cream, eggs and a jar of home-made jam, plus a Camp Coffee bottle full of the marvellous mint sauce, made to her own unique recipe, which she knew I loved. In addition to these delights she never, on any occasion, omitted to give me 2/- or 2/6d to cover the expense of the railway journey, accompanied by the warning, "Don't let your uncle see what you've got in that basket." In spite of her con-stant threats to "transmogrify" me, I treasure the memory of that kind-hearted woman with so warm a nature, hidden behind a cloak of asperity, and am glad to say she lived to a good old age.

Exeter Library

I was an avid reader at this time and a frequent visitor to the City Library in Queen Street. This had a Juvenile Section consisting of about two rows of books, at ground level, available for ratepayers' children under twelve years of age. I cannot honestly say that I recall any particular book: they must have been by authors such as Kipling, Henty, Fennimore Cooper and so on. Clearly I found them absorbing, since I had exhausted the contents of the Juvenile Section some time before I was twelve and was given the full reader's ticket by special dispensation.

Every book in the library was bound with stiff red covers - not a single coloured cover appeared on any of the shelves. The process of borrowing and returning books was essentially the same as today except that the dating and recording was all done by hand. The books were lent for a fortnight and the fine was one penny per week for a late return.

This free City Library was on the ground floor of the left-hand wing of the Museum in Queen Street. The Librarian at that time was Mr Tapley Soper, a very forbidding figure with a pronounced limp. Exonians owe the Library's inception to the imagination and fore-thought of a group of Councillors and the splendid support given to the project by the enthusiastic Conservative, Charles Westcombe, in the 1860s.

St Lukes College Practising School

While my parents were struggling with the problem of financing the business and furnishing so many extra rooms (usually by picking up odd "lots" for a few shillings at sales or second-hand shops), I had to start life at a new school: the St Luke's College Practising School on Heavitree Hill.

The atmosphere here was completely different from that of St John's and I rapidly acquired a sense of security and friendship. There was none of the fierce shouting and reckless football which had characterised play and meal times at St John's. The headmaster was Mr R I Partridge, known of course as "Rip", then in his fif-ties. There was no abrasiveness about him: he was quiet in his speech, gentle in his manner and had time to move around and talk to individual boys. I never saw a cane during the two years I spent there. Classes ran smoothly and quietly but with none of the drive and urgency of my previous years.

My particular form-master was Mr H H Hawkins, a large, refined and able teacher with an unusual egg-shaped head, or perhaps it was partial baldness which gave me the "egg" impression; in later years I believe he became the head of a Church of England Training College. From his hands I received the greatest of kindness and could approach him for help whenever it was needed.

The school was a free Church School; this fact, together with the small size of the classes and the characters of Mr Partridge and Mr Hawkins, probably explained the general happiness, so much a feature of those years. There was a junior section to this school, housed near the top of Paris Street, and probably this contributed to our quiet well-being, though it must have involved Mr Partridge in a fair amount of walking. The school derived its name from its location at the end of the St Luke's College buildings, our actual connection with the latter being confined to our use, literally, as a "practising" school; our classes were taken from time to time by students at St Luke's usually in the adjoining college buildings.

It soon became apparent that I was at least a year ahead of other boys in the class and accordingly I was sometimes given the task (a very pleasant one) of walking round and marking their arithmetic and pointing out errors where they were obvious.

I was due to sit the scholarship exam for Hele's School in June of 1914 and as the exam time drew near I was allowed to revise in a back seat whenever I found normal class work familiar. The scholarship examination, as I have mentioned, was in two parts and these I successfully passed but at the interview Mr F G Snowball, the headmaster of Hele's at that time, taking note of my size and age (10 years 9 months) suggested that it might be better for me to sit again in the following year. Thus I was given a second year at St Luke's obtaining my scholarship at the age of 11 years 9 months. When the result was announced, Mr Partridge made a point of congratulating me and telling me that this was the first scholarship the school had obtained. It was a happy conclusion to two very happy years.

John Stocker School - beginnings
Some six years later I revisited my first primary

52

school, St John's, and spoke for a moment or two to Mr Howells, who had succeeded Mr Smith as headmaster. He remarked, "Aren't you sorry you left this school when you did and that your name does not appear on our honours board?" It was only then that I realised he was ignorant of the fact that I had been asked to leave on account of non-payment of fees. It became clear later still that none of the staff had appreciated this, my withdrawal having been arranged by some official in the Education Office. By this time - about 1921 - all fee paying in the city's primary schools had been abolished.

Eventually St John's was absorbed into St Thomas School, which became known as the John Stocker School - a tribute to the work of the then Chairman of the Education Committee. In 1942 the buildings of St John's School were obliterated in the massive German air-raid on the night of June 6th.

The Higher Market in Queen Street

FIRST WORLD WAR - Making Ends Meet

Reverting to life at home, the financial position improved a little during 1914, my father having obtained

work as an orderly in the Eye Infirmary which had been converted into a Military Hospital. The pay, of course, was small but was supplemented occasionally by the biscuit tins of discarded cakes and bread-and-butter thrown out from the kitchens, which my father salvaged and brought home to us.

Buller watching the trams go by.

Topsham and Higher Barracks

In the early months of the war there was another unexpected increase, for a few weeks, in the household income. This arose from a sudden influx of soldiers, mostly recruits, into Exeter. They numbered far more than the Higher Barracks and the Topsham Barracks could cope with and compulsory billeting powers had to be

employed to secure sleeping accommodation for them. The Billeting Officer had a highly unpopular task to perform but the gentleman who called in due course at No 52 must have left with a smile on his face. He was welcomed by my parents, who promptly agreed to take six - two men (or lads) per room. As far as I remember, the billeting allowance was 7/- per man per week.

The military training given to these recruits was very brief: within a couple of months most were in France.

With a steadier inflow, the need for billeting was removed and life for us returned to normal.

Sidwell Street from the air.

Many people in Exeter made ends meet by caring for the abandoned misfits of society. For example a great-aunt of mine, who in her sixties and seventies ran a cafe at the top end of Sidwell Street, accepted responsibility for the care of a slightly sub-normal but quite harmless lady: her main abnormality was her insistence on wearing (as I was told) nothing but newspaper under her dress.

I used to visit this great-aunt fairly frequently on Saturday mornings: I could be certain of getting a cup of tea there and a doughnut which was nonetheless acceptable for its being usually nearly a week old. During the war years this aunt used to save the tea-leaves from the many individual cups of tea she sold, dry them and when she had filled a Woodbine box with them would pass them on for second use at No 52. We appreciated the thought.

A well-known High Street shop

West Quarter Children

Mother had at that time six children of her own to feed and clothe - I include my eldest sister Evelyn as one of the "children" but in fact she was a terrific worker, coping with the many household duties during Mother's bouts of bronchitis and asthma. Nevertheless, following an appeal from our church, St Mary Major, Mother agreed to take two more children into her fold: these were Danny and Lily Gurd, aged about five and seven respectively. They were two of a family of four children whose father was in Australia and whose mother had very recently died of cancer in the slum area of the West Quarter. This ensured a further 12/- a week (6/- per child) from the parish towards our combined expenses.

I remember the upheaval caused at No 52: the Gurd children had to be bathed, given fresh clothes and de-loused, a process involving in those days almost con-tinuous onslaughts with the "small tooth comb". We were all caught up in this to ensure no spread of lice occurred, each of us in turn having to kneel on the floor in the kitchen with head bent over a sheet of newspaper on Mother's lap while she operated the comb. There was of course no bathroom and all baths had to be taken in the kitchen in succession, with kettles and saucepans of hot water supplied by the kitchen range. In a few weeks Danny and Lily were duly absorbed into the family.

Some months later the vicar called again, explaining that the remaining two Gurds were unhappy at being separated from the others, whereupon the two older children, aged about nine and twelve, joined us as well. Luckily these two had been tended by another family in the intervening weeks and there were no problems of cleanliness to be overcome. Thus another 12/- per week was added to the budget.

Sleeping and Eating

There were now ten children in the household. I have no idea, looking back, as to the sleeping arrangements my parents made for so many, except that my brother and

I shared a bed in the top room, while the youngest Gurd, Danny, slept in a small bed in the same room. There were three other bedrooms - apart from the one occupied by our visitors - available for my parents, my baby brother and the six girls. I was too young and always too busy to be aware of the domestic arrangements.

The main problem, initially, must have been beds and bedding. I remember the bed my brother and I shared, with its single flock mattress laid on a criss-cross of metal springs; in cold weather most of our day clothes would be used as supplementary bedding.

In point of fact my youngest brother, Roy, took my place in the top bedroom more often than not. When the weather was

The famous Tudor House that later moved

fine I slept in the summer-house on the flat roof - always a tremendous thrill. From this high vantage point, with its metal parapet, one could get a clear view right away to the estuary of the Exe, towards

Topsham and Lympstone. On a moonlit night the silver thread of the river was clearly visible, while in the early morning the slopes of Haldon with the belvedere on the crest broke through the light white mist which enshrouded the distant miles of fruitful fields and farms. On other occasions I slept on the sofa in the sitting room; once or twice I tried the kitchen but found the top of the table a little precarious and the situation underneath it too claustrophobic. I should add that I was the prime instigator of these nocturnal changes; I was only too  delighted with the small excitements and the prospect of a later bedtime and used to overcome my parents' recurring anxieties by my protestations that I could sleep anywhere.

The load of work and organisation at home must have fallen on my father, my mother and Evelyn. I do not know how they managed the capital expenditure involved, small though it was. I remember one acquisition which came up the street from the second-hand shop: this was a long waiting-room seat from some railway station. No doubt it had once been well-padded but by the time it reached us the springs had gone and it sagged badly. It stretched along the whole of one side of the kitchen and could take five children easily. Being the eldest boy, I'm glad to relate that I never had to sit upon it. Mother sat at one end of the large kitchen table and the rest of us used a couple of chairs and a form. Mother kept a cane on the mantelpiece within easy reach: it was never used but its message was plain. As a family I cannot recall disagreements or squabbles among the children; our greatest enemy was "the giggles" and my parents must have shown great forbearance when these attacks occurred. One threat which could restore order was to be "sent to the cellar", though that in fact only meant standing on the top stair until the giggles had subsided.

Mother was an expert cook. From a sheep's head she could make a first-class brawn; the tongue, skinned and set in a small container, provided an extra delicacy, as did the brains, fried and served on toast. She could turn out a marvellous soup based on a sixpenny marrowbone and a packet of bright yellow split peas with potatoes, doughboys and onions. On no occasion did we ever have a big joint; there was sometimes a special feature supplied by a rabbit or boiling fowl.

If Mother wanted mutton she sent for mutton, if she needed a cheap fowl she would ask for a boiling fowl, in other words an old hen: the silly, sweeping terms "lamb" and "chicken" hadn't arrived for us.

Rice puddings, spotted dick with custard, Cornish pasties, herrings (7 for 6d) purchased at the door when in season, all contributed to a balanced diet. We obtained our milk from Callard's Dairy across the road, fetched in jugs of course, though relations there became strained when Mother decided to sell cream, obtaining seven-pound tins from, I think, the Somerset Dairy. It must have contained some preservative, for it always lasted many days; probably this purchase was made from time to time more on our behalf than on possible customers', since it was bought on wholesale terms.

Mother's slogan was "one good meal a day"; she stuck most rigidly to this rule and saw that it was maintained even if she were ill. Somehow, at least as far as the children were concerned, there seemed never any panic as regards our food supply. I remember just one morning, and only one, on which I was told "There is nothing but bread for breakfast this morning." I was given two slices of bread which were cut into small, neat squares and placed in a large cup; boiling water was poured over this and salt and pepper sprinkled thereon - "salt and

60

pepper broth". I clearly remember that I regarded this in the nature of an experiment in breakfast food. There was absolutely no feeling of distress or of poverty and in fact, as a family, we never felt that there was anything unusual about our diet.

I have no doubt my parents found the continuous struggle frustrating and at times depressing but as far as the rest of us were concerned, we were never aware of any provisioning difficulties. We were never, ever unhappy on this score and for the greater part of our early and teenage years we were never even conscious of any deprivation.

My father had many of his meals at the hospital, his hours of duty being at times continuous and unpredictable. When a hospital train arrived in the city, fleets of "ambulances" - often just lorries - carried the wounded to the various hospitals. My father would then, acting as one of the stretcher-bearers, convey the patients to the wards where the doctors and nurses took over. These arrivals often happened at night, hence the unpredictability of the hours. Incidentally, "overtime" was another word like "lamb" and "chicken" - not yet in common use.

It all comes out in the wash!

One major household chore was of course the laundry. In one corner of the cellar there was a large copper and, in another corner, a tap. Having filled the copper with water and then covered it with a large wooden top, the fire would be lit underneath it; this was an operation undertaken by my father or Evelyn around 6.30 a.m. each Monday morning. From about 8.30 to 12.00 a whole mass of sheets, pillowslips, towels and clothes would be brought to the boil, individual attention being given on the way, where necessary, by means of a ridged scrubbing board and scrubbing brush. They were then transferred in turn from the copper to a large tin bath, where they were rinsed before being passed through the two rollers of a mangle. I remember still Mother's shrunken hands when she emerged from the cellar after these Monday sessions.

Drying was a problem shared by everybody in the house. There were clothes-lines on the top landing and sheets of paper were laid on the level banisters, each some three yards long, on each of the three floors; over these were draped the many sheets, shirts and so on, until the whole house seemed saturated. Drying on occasion would take a number of days, to be followed by a massive ironing campaign with the aid of a metal iron which was heated on the gas.

Incidentally, this use of the banisters in time removed their polish, which led ultimately to a last-minute revarnishing session by my father and me two days before my sister's wedding. For good measure we also varnished the table in our front room which was to be used for the reception lunch of the bridesmaids and guests. Unfortunately, it was midwinter and precious little of the wretched varnish dried in time. On the wedding morning we had to cover the table top with newspapers, most of which remained as a permanent feature. There were some very caustic remarks and one or two very black looks as the important visitors dis-covered the inevitable stains on some of their finery; in some cases it took more than one glass of rum or port to restore normality.

Pearce's Rag and Bone Dealers

Further points of interest occur to me here. At the bottom of Magdalen Street, a yard or two up the little Trinity Street, were the premises of a rag-and-bone dealer by the name of Pearce. I was often grateful to that store for the penny, or sometimes tuppence, which was obtainable on a good rabbit skin. For those interested in fishing, maggots could be bought there for a song.

The City of Exeter has cause also to be grateful to Mr Pearce, for on one occasion there came to him for des-truction a large box of old papers. On examination he found these to be manuscripts relating to purchases, sales, legal proceedings and so on referring to a cer-tain Holbrook Farm and Estate in the parish of Honiton Clyst; the seals on some of these documents alone were of great interest and value. Instead of sending the mass of paper to be pulped, Mr Pearce transferred it to the City and it is now one of many treasured items in the Record Office in Castle Street.

As must be becoming clear, with my father working and a room or two being let, financial problems diminished and Mother was able to begin building up the stocks of cigarettes and tobacco. Confectionery, too, became more evident in the "swan" window but this brought its own problem - the invasion of the shop by ants.

It was no advertisement for the business for a possible purchaser, on inspecting the luscious toffees and chocolates spread out for his or her enticement, to perceive an army of ants sampling them with evident enthusiasm. Some deterrent was essential and this, mercifully, was found: a very fine dusting of all the cracks in the floor of the window and along the edges of the wainscotting below it with DDT proved amazingly effective. The ants disappeared and were never seen in any quantity again. Curiously enough, two days later the lady of the house next door, when making some small purchases, remarked that her kitchen had suddenly been over-run by thousands of ants; "Where they have come from," she said, "I've no idea!" Mother sympathised but, I fear, did not dwell on the point.

In the spring of 1914 and successive years pea and bean sticks became part of the stock in trade. These were purchased, a load at a time, direct from farms, perhaps a dozen or fifteen bundles of each. Somehow they were crammed into the shop, the greatest of care having to be used to avoid the electric

lights. One bundle of each would be tied securely to the outside of the shop, with the prices clearly marked: 6d for the pea sticks and 9d for the bean sticks at first, though later the prices rose to 9d and 1/-. Luckily there was a ready sale for these and the worst of the jam was usually over in a couple of days; later the prices rose again to 1/- and 1/6d.

With these occasional additions to profits Mother decided to purchase a piano; she herself had learnt to play as a child at Lympstone and Evelyn had had several years' tuition prior to 1912. The piano came from Godfrey's in Bridge Street and cost Mother 2/6d a week for between three and four years. It went into the sitting-room above the shop.

1915 ushered in a few years of even greater financial stability since in due course my father was called into the Services. Separation Allowances became payable, while a Civil Liabilities Tribunal granted Mother the sum of £30 per annum as part-compensation for my father's withdrawal from the business.

Then in 1916 Mother noticed convalescent soldiers streaming past the house just after 2.00 p.m. each day, being allowed out - if fit - for the afternoon. She put two or three chairs and a small table in one corner of the shop with a tablecloth, cups, saucers and plates, purchased a few cakes and put a notice in the window: just one word "TEAS". This proved an immediate boon to the wounded; soon there were half-a-dozen regulars, three or four round the table and two or three seated on the stairs on the other side of the shop leading to the hall. Mother made the tea in the kitchen and Evelyn dashed to and fro serving it. The numbers grew almost daily until between 2.00 and 2.30 any afternoon the shop would be crowded with Australians, while still more sat on the stairs leading to the bedrooms. Our sitting-room was converted into a tea-room and within a few weeks that too was crowded. For Mother and Evelyn it was a wild rush which lasted, usually, only about half an hour before the visitors wandered off into the city. It added a few shillings' profit to the day's takings and enabled the stock of cigarettes and confectionery to be

64

increased still further.

Except during the holidays, we children missed all this: by late afternoon each day, on our return from school, we would find our tea ready and the house as calm as usual. At that time a customer entering the shop could never be certain of what he might find: a forest of sticks with the narrowest of gaps from door to counter and from counter to kitchen; or a shop, hall and stairs packed with soldiers balancing cups of tea precariously as they chattered or roared out "Waltzing Matilda"; or, on the contrary, he might find a shop practically empty of stock and having only a diminutive child in charge.

Such was probably the case one day when the vicar of St Thomas, Mr Prince, arrived; my parents had formerly been his parishioners. He turned up complete with silk top hat and frock coat, evidently making a routine call which was not repeated.

We also had regular weekly visits from insurance agents intent on collecting their weekly thruppence, sixpence or ninepence which covered the fire hazard or the possible death of a relative, near or distant. In those days you could insure practically anyone for very small sums of money; there was one occasion, some years later, when Mother was paid £8 following somebody's death. It was a strain meeting those constant raids on the till: with great difficulty one might gather together perhaps three or four shillings in the course of the day, only to see 1/- or 1/6d of it disappear quite unexpectedly. Payments were entered in ruled notebooks, similar to those used by the Post Office or Building Societies today, and there were always four or five pink or yellow cards or books standing at the end of the kitchen mantelpiece. These collectors were for the most part patient and pleasant though there was one, Mr James, bowler-hatted and bearded, who would bluster and abuse Mother if no payment were forthcoming when he called: a noisy, unpleasant bully was Mr James.

As a till, Mother acquired an ancient second-hand folding writing desk or "escritoire". There was a long secret drawer at the bottom which we found packed with letters of a bygone generation. Many of these letters were written on lace-edged paper and the writing ran both horizontally and vertically, in other words the paper had been turned through a right-angle and the letter continued across what had already been written. With the stupidity or ignorance of the period, after noting that the writers were not local people, these treasures of the past were destroyed. This was, no doubt, only one of many acts of vandalism of which we were unknowingly guilty.

I recall, for example, that just at that period I acquired one of the very first horn and cylinder gramophones, with half a dozen Edison Bell records.

The original owner of this had been an elderly lady living in the St Leonard's area, Mrs Widgery, who, for a small fee, told fortunes. About twice a year she was invited for an hour to No 52. She and Mother would retire to the tea-room upstairs and there, with the aid of a pack of cards, they looked into the future. A hush always fell upon the house during these proceedings and those of us old enough to know what was going on would wait anxiously downstairs for the verdict. Was it a marriage? Was money on its way, associated with a dark man? Were there signs of trouble? Or, most dreaded of all, was there a funeral in sight? Mother's face would be scanned anxiously when at the end of the fortune-telling she came downstairs to make the inevitable cup of tea and sandwich for the visitor.

Mother bought the gramophone from Mrs Widgery for 2/6d and this innovation was enjoyed for a time. Then the little driving belt linking the motor (wound up by hand) with the cylinder broke. I tried string of various thicknesses as a substitute but this was not successful, so that relic too, in due course, went into the dustbin.

Foggy Exeter

November fogs in Exeter, though occasional events, were to be dreaded by asthma sufferers. I remember one particular fog, yellowish-brown in colour, which was, in our neighbourhood, quite impenetrable. The district became eerily silent, with vision restricted literally to about a yard. No such thing as a "smokeless zone" was heard of in those days and thousands of coal fires had contributed that particular night to the literally breath-taking density of what would otherwise have been a normal white mist from the Exe.

Hele's School Days

I moved to Hele's School in 1915. In addition, I was preoccupied at that time with two other extensions to my life, those of chorister and scout. During one of the vicar's visits to No 52 in the early summer of 1915 it was arranged that I should attend an audition with the choirmaster and organist (Mr W V Cole) of St Mary Major Church. I was accepted and became a choirboy forthwith at what was then the very satisfying figure of 4/- per quarter; in later years this rose to 5/-. In all, I remained a choirboy for over six years. Attendance at church naturally brought me to the notice of the curate, the Reverend J A S Castlehow, and in a very short time I found myself also a member of the local troop of scouts under his leadership. From this period onwards, for the next seven years, practically every minute of my spare time was devoted either to choir practices and church services or to scouting.

A choirboy strike at St Mary Major

As far as the choir is concerned, I have few memories of note. I do recall that the quarterly pay-days were often heavily delayed, culminating round about 1918 or 1919 in a choirboys' strike of which, of course, the parents knew nothing until it had happened and the Sunday evening service was held without the support of the boys. We were individually and collectively severely reprimanded for this unheard-of behaviour. It was never repeated but we observed that from that time the boys were paid with considerably more promptitude.

68

The Ever-busy High Street

I recall also one vigorous, outspoken sermon by the vicar in which he complained bitterly of those parishioners who spent often 4d or 6d a day on cigarettes but yet could find only 1d for the Sunday collection: "Three and sixpence a week for smoking," he thundered, "and one penny only for St Mary Major!" One realises now what tremendous strains were involved in the upkeep of this church; it was in fact one of two serving this parish, the other, a smaller church, being that of St Mary Magdalene situated at the centre of the poorest and most overcrowded part of the city of Exeter.

69

Pennsylvania's Golf Links

Mr Castlehow was tremendously keen on camping and, in the spring of 1915, he had obtained permission from the farmer concerned for the erection of a summer standing camp. This was situated on the very high ground at the edge of a strip of woodland which marked the most distant end of what was then the Exeter Golf Links. From this vantage point one could survey miles of the Exe valley with river, road and railway far below. Across the valley stood the little hills of Exwick, Upton Pyne, the Raddon Hills and Thorverton, disappearing in the distance through Stoke Canon towards Silverton and Tiverton; on many a summer morning I have seen the tips of those hills emerging like distant islands in an ocean of white mist.

Three "bell" tents were erected along this ridge, one for Mr Castlehow, one for working boys and the third for schoolboys. Each evening, unless the weather made it quite impossible, members of St Mary Major's scout troop walked the two or three miles from Exeter up the five hundred foot height of Pennsylvania, passing on their way near the top the lovely row of white and gleaming Georgian houses in Pennsylvania Park. These overlooked nearly the whole of Exeter and the distant silvery estuary of the Exe, flanked by Haldon on one side and Woodbury Common on the other.

Just outside the Park there was a welcome seat and on very many occasions I stopped at that point, not only to rest but to observe an exceedingly active and noisy rookery which was established in a fine group of tall trees on the opposite side of the road.

The route continued past Duryard (entry to this estate cost 1d) to the Golf Links entrance and then across the Links to the camp. We all took sandwiches and a supply of tea and sugar, a camp fire was lit, supper enjoyed and then after prayers we dispersed to our tents.

The troop possessed one somewhat battered bugle and on this someone nightly sounded - or attempted to sound - "Lights Out" round about 9.30 p.m. It was an ear-splitting and usually hilarious nightcap; in the seven years during which I enjoyed these summer camps the troop never once boasted even a reasonable bugle player.

The working boys were roused at 5 a.m.; most of them worked at Willeys Iron Foundry in St Thomas's and had to be at work by 6 o'clock. The fortunate schoolboys were called at 7 a.m.; I usually arrived home at about 7.45 in good time for a clean-up, breakfast and school.

There are two or three particular events I recall. One was when a would-be "wit" dropped a stink-bomb at nightfall into Mr Castlehow's tent. It being obviously a schoolboy action he came straight to our tent, made us pack all our belongings, fold up our ground sheets and then roll up the sides of his bell tent and transfer ourselves lock, stock and barrel to his tent while he prepared to take ours. By the time the changeover had been completed all traces of sulphuretted hydrogen had disappeared, whereupon he decided to move us all back again: all this by starlight and one flickering hurricane lamp!

Fire at Stoke Canon

On another occasion, when Mr Castlehow was serving as chaplain in Northern France, we were awakened by his deputy Mr C E Purves at about 3 a.m. when he had spotted a red glow some mile or so away in the valley below. We all hastily pulled on boots and coats and made our way down across the dew-soaked field to the nearest gate and so to the Stoke Canon Road.

We found the paper mills at Stoke Canon ablaze from end to end, with a mass of flames and showers of sparks shooting into the night sky. Of course we offered our services officially to the officer in charge of the Fire Brigade and quite naturally we were told just to keep

71

out of the way.   I was, however, lucky in that I was given the task of fetching, for one of the fire-fighters, a warm coat from his cottage in the village half a mile away.   For this service, duly accomplished, I gratefully received a cup of tea drawn from the bucket which was being passed round from one fireman to another.   Even now I recall how acceptable that hot drink was!   When it was light we climbed the hill back to camp and so home.

Another night, a puzzled and enquiring cow pushed its head into our tent.   That part was easy but withdrawing it was quite a different matter.   It cost us several hours of hard sewing to repair the resultant rents in the fabric so that the tent became once more rainproof.

Then   there   was a night during which we   had   a   most terrific thunderstorm.   We must have been right at its centre, with the beating of the rain on the sides of the tent, the repeated claps and rolls of thunder and the vivid flashes of lightning which showed, every few seconds, the white-faced schoolboys peeping from beneath their blankets.   It seemed never-ending but suddenly the figure of Mr Purves slithered in under the tent flaps. He remarked as casually as he could in the din, "I think we might offer up a prayer on such a night as this." Appealing for divine protection, together we said the Lord's Prayer with a deep and anxious "Amen" at the end. Never was prayer answered so swiftly.   Within moments the storm died down, the thunder rolled off into the distance and quite solemn silence descended on our rather bedraggled group.   A few more words of reassur-ance before Mr Purves retired to his own tent and within minutes we were all asleep once more.

Those nightly camps became part of my life: school during the day, an hour's homework and then, suitably armed with sandwiches and tea, once more off to Pennsylvania. During the years 1915-21 most of us spent anything from eighty to a hundred nights annually under canvas.

Sir Robert Newman - MP for Exeter

In 1915, as a contribution to the War effort, we were asked to cut bracken, to be used as a substitute for hay for the army. At that time horses were used not only, of course, for cavalry units but for all manner of transport. Arrangements were made for the scouts, some twenty in number, to camp in Mamhead Park during the first ten days of August, at the invitation of Sir Robert Newman, later Lord Mamhead. Alas, however, when we had pitched camp and settled in ready for work it was found that there were no implements available for our use. Our war service, on that occasion, fizzled out to everybody's chagrin. The only bracken we cut was with our scout knives, gathering sufficient to form a thick layer in each tent upon which we spread our ground sheets and blankets at bedtime.

I always found the smell of this bracken thoroughly un- pleasant during the first night of camp: it had a sickly, per- vasive odour when green but this became less noticeable on the second night and forgotten thereafter.

We had a most glorious week's camp, one which we were very kindly allowed to repeat for each of the six suc- ceeding years. The first Wednesday of that week in 1915 was an Open Day. Parents had been invited to the Park; there were races and jumps in the grounds in front of Mamhead House, after which prizes were awarded. We all then proceeded to take tea as Sir Robert's guests on the terrace, enjoying at the same time the magnificent view over the surrounding countryside to the Exe estuary and the blue waters of Dawlish and the Warren, a setting planned and executed by Capability Brown.

The company, I remember, included not only Sir Robert

but also his sister and brother-in-law, Mr and Mrs Lumley, and a stately visitor called Mrs Ratcliffe. Very much worthy of note was the impressive and dignified butler who waited upon us with a welcoming smile and with whom we were to become even better acquainted in the succeeding years.

Later we were allowed to climb to the top of the castle tower: this was in fact a picturesque addition to the house forming part of the stable buildings and erected, I believe, at the same time as the house by Sir Robert Newman's father, a wealthy wool merchant from Plymouth. I discovered that Sir Robert had earlier given Mr Castlehow a pound note and with this he had purchased sufficient prizes for the winners of the sports events (such as they were) as well as consolation prizes for the remaining scouts in the troop, so that we all came away with something (even me!) the boys returning to camp and the parents setting out for the three-mile walk to Starcross station.

made in readiness for the camp.

Bit of a Jam!

The cost of these camps was met by a weekly contribution during the year of 1d, together with a 5/- charge for the week. Mother from the outset paid my 5/- in the form of jam: apple, blackberry, pear, vegetable marrow and a pound or two of apricot, plum, raspberry, gooseberry, black and red currant - as these fruits arrived on the market in bulk they were purchased and the jams made We usually provided between thirty and forty pounds of mixed jams for that week. I remember Mr Castlehow saying one day, "I don't know what your Mother puts into this jam but it is certainly good stuff!"

My father being a butcher, I had early learnt to skin and prepare a rabbit, and rabbits in fact gave us two or three grand stews for the simple reason that a kindly gamekeeper provided us with as many as we could consume for the price of the shots he'd fired: this was never more than a penny a rabbit.

The evening meal was always the main meal of the day but our breakfasts too were quite satisfying events, consisting of large helpings of porridge and treacle, followed by as much bread and jam and tea as we could consume. Each day a particular Patrol was responsible for the catering and for supplying the camp with milk and water from somewhat distant farms. The porridge for breakfast was prepared on the previous evening: it was brought slowly to the boil, care being taken to keep it stirred to avoid burning, and was then placed in a large box and packed round with hay. By morning it needed only a few minutes' re-heating before being served. I remember only one occasion when breakfast was a failure. That year we had with us one lad, "Spider", with a pronounced chip on his shoulder. He disliked camp intensely and hated work of any kind even more. When it was his turn to prepare breakfast he threw Quaker Oats into the huge billy-can, filled the latter with water and put it on the camp fire, ignoring all instructions about slow heating and stirring. Next morning when it was taken from the hay box we found practically a solid mass of burnt porridge and a ruined container! It was bread and jam that morning. Half an hour later our disgruntled Spider found himself on his way home - to our great relief and, I suspect, to his.

Except for the Duty Patrol, most days provided opportunities for bathing excursions to Dawlish, Dawlish Warren or Teignmouth. Each of these resorts was about four miles from Mamhead and in the course of time and with the aid of a large-scale map we were able to find certain field paths and lanes which shortened the journeys. We usually had a few coppers to spend on these occasions; one year I remember receiving a windfall from home mid-week in the form of a postal order for 1/6d, at that time a very large addition to one's pocket money.

Once or twice, armed with tin mugs we climbed through the Park towards the obelisk gathering whortleberries or bilberries, ostensibly for a pie: this never materialised. When we returned to camp the blue stains on our faces and fingers revealed some success in our mission but these tiny fruit were so tedious to gather that it was easier to dispose of them on the spot rather than attempt to fill a mug.

Of the seven camps at Mamhead Park in which I took part, Mr Castlehow organised and supervised five. Of the remaining two camps, one was run by Mr Purves and the other by Mr Grenfell, the Head of the Rack Street Primary School located at the centre of the overcrowded area of Exeter, known as the West Quarter, which formed the parish of St Mary Major.

Of the boys who were my camp companions I recall principally one Bill Blackman. He was about two years my senior, working at Willeys Foundry when I first knew him; he was a natural leader, an extrovert with a cheerful, willing attitude to any task on hand. His high spirits led him on one occasion, when Mr Castlehow was in France and other authority temporarily absent, to form a band. A huge tin bath was used as a drum, while tin plates, metal saucepans and our outworn bugle constituted the other instruments. Thus equipped, and with appropriate vocal accompaniment of wartime songs, the "band" paraded around Mamhead Park. It may have been a "Long, Long Way from Tipperary" but it wandered far too close to Mamhead House. There was no complaint made at the time but some months later Mr Castlehow made a pointed reference to the escapade.

Bill Blackman was in fact a very able scout, becoming in due course a King's Scout. I followed his example in this but it took me some three years to qualify, chiefly on account of the fifty-yards swimming test. One could, as I have mentioned, get practice in swimming at the Exeter Baths at a cost of sixpence per visit but very few sixpences were available so I had to do most of my "training" in the River Exe at Stafford's Bridge (between Stoke Canon and Exeter and not far from Cowley Bridge) round about 7.00 a.m., on my way home from camp to Southernhay.

Another popular pastime - boating on the Exeter Canal at the Double Locks

The last condition for the First Class Badge was to have one shilling in a Savings Bank. I remember that on the day I obtained a Swimming Certificate, Mother lent me a shilling and I duly secured a Post Office Savings Book with one shilling to my credit, so I was able to produce both that same evening. I withdrew the shilling the next day and returned it!

I was grateful to one of the scouts for a week's

employment in 1916. He had taken a post as a general help to a family living in one of the large houses in Southernhay, working in the basement from 6.30 to 7.30 each morning from Monday to Saturday on such chores as shoe-cleaning and cutlery and brass polishing, for 2/6d a week. I was glad of the half-crown when I received it but just one week of rising at 6.00 a.m. was enough for me and I was glad when my friend had finished his holiday and returned to his early morning pre-school employment!

I did not own a bicycle until 1919 but there existed a bicycle shop, Warne's, in Magdalen Street in premises next to the "Valiant Soldier" and it was possible to hire a machine there at 6d for an hour or 9d for two hours.

I was indebted to Sir Robert of Mamhead for a "Recommend" to the Eye Infirmary in Magdalen Street; this was a slip of paper given to subscribers to the hospital's upkeep entitling them to nominate patients for free treatment. With one of these signed by Sir Robert I obtained a consultation and a pair of steel-rimmed spectacles in my last year at school. There was, of course, no NHS at that time and many people in fact selected their own spectacles by trial and error from the dozens of specimen pairs available for purchase at a domestic bazaar at a price, I think of 6d.

Cathedral Close

The 1914-18 war did of course affect us all closely. In the course of the four years most members of the scout troop had relatives wounded or killed and as the demand for reinforcements abroad grew more urgent, so compulsory military service was introduced, age limits for calling-up were raised and few families were unaffected.

As far as the troop was concerned, after the abortive bracken expedition we turned our attention to the collection of waste paper. The City rented basement premises under Veitch's (seedsmen, etc.) in Cathedral Close. A committee of ladies was organised to weigh and sort out all the books, papers and manuscripts which could be gathered from the loyal citizens of Exeter and these were then despatched to appropriate factories for re-pulping. Anyone with spare paper of any kind either called with their addresses or sent post-cards to the Cathedral Close depot. It was then our task - that is the task of schoolboy scouts - to take a ·trek-cart to the addresses supplied by the ladies, returning to the Close when we had completed the list. There were iron gratings in the pavement outside Veitch's and our load of salvage was passed through them to the willing hands beneath.

To Peamore House

I recall that there was a Scout Badge which could be won by any lad who spent a hundred days of three hours each in this collection effort; several of us duly obtained these service badges. There was also a reward for any scout troop which collected one hundred tons of paper for the war effort: this consisted of a brand new trek-cart, the latest model of its kind, which could be assembled from its component parts in a matter of minutes. It took our particular group, I think, about two and a half years to earn that trek-cart but we did get it, to our great jubilation!

In the course of the war years I visited nearly every part of the city on these jaunts but the one that I remember most clearly was that which two of us made with the trek-cart to collect a load from Peamore House one afternoon. We were received by Lady Kekewich, accepting with alacrity her invitation to join her at tea before returning to Exeter. Before leaving she presented each of us with three magnificent peacock's feathers which I took home and gave to Mother with great pride and delight: they really were most beautiful. However, as soon as Mother saw them she drew back and in no uncertain terms told me to throw them away or get rid of them immediately, she didn't want such unlucky things in the house!

Royal Clarence Hotel
Another event has remained vividly in my memory and that was being shown the first-floor room of the paper depot in the Close. This was large and high and lined with mirrors from the wainscot to within a foot of the cornice. Gorgeous candelabra hung from the ceiling, while around the walls and immediately above the mirrors were quite a large number of colourful coats of arms. It was a memorable experience to stand in that empty room with the light switched on and to see countless images reflected from one mirror to its opposite companion.

Recently, in the search for a particular coat of arms belonging to a former Freeman of the city, one Abraham Rutter, I visited what had been Veitch's for fifty years or more and was told that the premises were now owned by the Royal Clarence Hotel. The receptionist there informed me that she knew every room in the hotel and there was none even remotely answering to my description: it had evidently been stripped and sub-divided into smaller separate rooms.

Deller's Cafe
With the end of the war the depot closed and I was given tea at Deller's Cafe by Mrs Passmore, the leader throughout of the little band of ladies who laboured week after week in the basement sorting, tying and weighing the heavy piles of paper for despatch to the Midlands. Incidentally, particular tribute was paid to the work of the schoolboy scouts and wolf-cubs of St Mary Major, the Mint and St David's in a report published in the *Express and Echo* on 26 November 1918 of a meeting of the Exeter Scouts Association.

My early years at Hele's School were thus intensely busy ones. Homework, I fear, received far less time and attention from me than was its due on many occasions, competing as it did with the claims of scouts and choir. There were, for example, scout meetings on several nights during autumn and winter, the headquarters consisting of the long attic of the wooden Church House which straddled the entrance from Sun Street into Mermaid Yard. We met usually from 7.30 to 9.30 in the evening; the first one and a half hours were devoted to work but the last half-hour was one of relaxation. In the course of the first period we worked for scout badges, checked and repaired where necessary tents and equipment which would be required in the ensuing summer, and so on. During the last half-hour, under Mr Castlehow's supervision, we were introduced over the years to draughts, chess, games of patience and later to auction bridge.

Follett Buildings - just around the corner from Mermaid Yard

Mr Castlehow had read mathematics at Selwyn College, Cambridge before taking Orders and throughout his life he was a keen chess and bridge player. Without being in the least conscious of his care or being grateful for the hours he spent on our behalf, the troop accepted his labours as a matter of course and right. During his years as Scoutmaster he must have cycled many hundreds of miles finding camp sites, arranging for instructors or badge examiners or merely in travelling additional journeys from camp to Exeter and back in the fulfilment of his normal parochial duties.

He lived with his mother in Bartholomew Street, to which on rare occasions Patrol Leaders were invited for discussion and planning; such meetings always concluded with tea and cakes produced by his widowed mother.

Mr Castlehow was a natural disciplinarian and a man of few words, a fact which as boys we appreciated enormously when he preached at St Mary Major. I regret that the common reaction to his efforts was usually one of antipathy, not at all on personal grounds but merely because in our eyes he represented Authority - with a capital "A" - and as such was regarded with distrust, especially by the working boys. He seemed to accept all this as natural and was entirely unmoved by the lack of cordiality extended at times to him.

In later years, as time rolled on, his work among us became more and more appreciated. I know that he kept in contact throughout his life with most of the boys whom he had first met as scouts. In the early 1920s he accepted a living at Witheridge, near Crediton, carrying on there the good work he had so ably performed in Exeter.

Meanwhile, back at Hele's School

While scouting filled my leisure hours during the years 1915-18, the more serious business of life occupied my days at Hele's School. Entering as a Scholar in a group of about twenty-five boys, I met Mr F G Snowball who combined the teaching of history and geography to certain forms with his duties as Headmaster. I admired him immensely; he was a big man but approachable and tremendously interested in early history. I still recall his initial lessons.

In one of the first, he produced a collection of early British implements - axe-heads and spear-heads with the flint shaping marks still visible - to supplement the text of the school book which he himself had written; I imagine he had borrowed a selection from the Exeter Museum authorities.

Again within the first two or three weeks we were asked by him to acquire a copy of the local one-inch Ordnance Survey Map. It was the first time that I had ever seen or owned such a treasure and I was absolutely fascinated to see so many familiar details spread before me; map-reading became immediately a satisfying pleasure which has remained with me throughout my life.

The Science Master at that time was Mr W Littler, who also introduced me to the mysteries of algebra and geometry. He was an efficient, matter-of-fact teacher. A feature of his science lessons was his insistence on the clear description of the experiments undertaken: the

aim, method and results had to be neatly written up in the last portion of the practical lessons, this task being finished off as homework and handed in the following day, when it was promptly marked and returned.

French was taught by Mr E Duhamel Cooke, nicknamed by us "Enamel", of course. He was to us the most popular assistant on the staff and we were delighted when he became our house-master. I think his secret lay in his more friendly, less formal approach to his work so that we felt much more at ease with him than with others. I remember just one outburst from him during a French lesson concerning the pronunciation of the simple word "de": "You Devonians are hopeless!" he cried, "Durr, durr, durr." I am reminded of a somewhat similar experience I endured when I first taught in Nottingham, where the figure one hundred and eleven came out as "woon, woon, woon"!

Mr Weston was my first Latin master. Irascible and strict, he found teaching Devon boys more than tedious at times: I remember him exclaiming one day at the top of his voice (which could frequently be heard far beyond the confines of his classroom) "Oh Lord deliver me from these fools of boys!" Except for the few years immediately following, when he was in the army, I fear he was not delivered until he retired.

On one occasion I recall being terrified when a certain member of my class complained to him that I was being helped in my work by someone outside the school. To my intense relief, Mr Weston simply said, "I'm very glad to hear it; you can all get as much help outside as you wish." I am happy to record that he lived to a very ripe old age, in spite of those early trials. He was temporarily succeeded by one of the women members who joined the staff as wartime replacements in 1916: this was Miss Jay - youthful, happy and enthusiastic.

A second lady was Mrs Houghton, older and more sedate; I have forgotten her particular subject, possibly it was English. She persuaded us to keep our minds on the task in hand by promising a special book prize for the best work. In due course, no doubt by some fluke, I qualified for this prize; unfortunately Mrs Houghton continually forgot to produce the book. One the last day of term I reminded her gently of the award. She very kindly apologised and gave me her address in Richmond Road so that I could collect it on the following afternoon. On calling, as arranged, I found she had left the city!

A great friend of mine was Fred White, who lent me his football boots on a number of occasions when circumstances compelled me to turn out for my House. In my time there were four of these Houses and the particular one you were in depended on the part of the city in which you resided. "South House" included Southernhay with not a footballer, as far as I remember, anywhere in its area: it had to scrape the barrel even to get a team together. I remember the approximate results of the three matches in which I played: two were lost in the region of 30 - 0 and the third lost 45 - 0! We thus established a record that is, I gather, still unbroken. The football field overlooked Cowley Bridge and had a very pronounced slope.

There was one unpleasant pupil at the school who set up a private enquiry business. We discovered one day that he possessed an exercise book with a page devoted to each individual member of the form. He had recorded every item of information he could gather about our parents and relatives and their past life and history. When completed the book was apparently passed round; although I didn't see it, I was told that it gave a faithful account of my father's bankruptcy some years earlier. At some stage the news spread further and we had a sharp lecture from Mr Snowball on the laws of libel. That lad should have joined the police force - he would have risen high in the ranks of the C.I.D.! Anyway he left us shortly afterwards, when his mother moved to Plymouth where in due course he became a chemist.

Another serious address, I remember, was given by the Headmaster in 1916 or 1917. It was at the time when the submarine blockade was at its most critical and the supply of food a matter of anxiety. The whole school assembled in the Hall: we were told to avoid waste at all costs and to get the full benefit of whatever we ate by chewing it at least sixteen times. I must have been highly impressionable - I find I'm still the last to finish a meal no matter with whom I dine!

Exeter's Bicycling Bishop

I enjoyed my journeys to and from Hele's as much as I had those explorations made between St John's Hospital School and my home in Church Road, St Thomas. The

direct route from Southernhay to Hele's at that time passed beneath the Burnett Patch foot-bridge to Cathedral Close and St Martin's lane but in later years it was possible to take a short cut from the D & E Hospital, through the Palace grounds to the Cathedral Close. We owed this to, I think, Lord William Cecil who was then Bishop of Exeter. He found the upkeep of the Palace and grounds heavy and lived towards the end of his episcopate in a more modest dwelling a little way above Cowley Bridge; incidentally, thereafter he was often seen on his yellow bicycle riding to and from the cathedral. The Palace gardens were then thrown open to the general public: many an Exonian unable to walk any great distance found tranquillity in that rather small but lovely garden with its beautiful trees, set between the Roman wall and the Palace.

Trinity Green

At that time, too, Trinity Green immediately opposite the hospital could be enjoyed by local residents and children.   It had originally been a burial ground but the headstones had been lifted and re-set along the enclosing walls, so leaving a central clear grassy space. On the side opposite the hospital, along Trinity Lane, there were a number of small cottage-like houses. All these houses have now disappeared and been replaced by large and rather ugly utilitarian sheds, obscuring completely the Roman wall behind them. The burial ground too has gone and is now the site of a concrete car park and a large public convenience.

Incidentally, when Dr Mortimer became Bishop of Exeter the Palace gardens were closed again and the privilege enjoyed by local inhabitants was withdrawn. No doubt this was advantageous to the Cathedral Authorities but their use was greatly missed and one hopes that the time may come when these gardens are once more open to the public.

Northernhay Park

Unless pressed for time I rarely came home by the direct route, sometimes using Northernhay, Rougemont Gardens, Castle Street, Bedford Circus and so to Southernhay and at other times coming by way of Queen Street, the full length of Northernhay, the Arcade and Southernhay East. In spring this latter was particu- larly pleasant: one could take a quick glance at the goldfish, skirt Northernhay with its masses of daffodils and primroses, on the slopes above what was then Queen Street Station, and - greatest thrill of all - one could use the footbridge over the railway lines in the station to pass from Northernhay through the station yard almost to the clock tower.

These homeward journeys also included trips along Richmond Road to Pepys Lane, a long descent by way of a succession of steps, from St David's Hill to Bonhay Road

The Deerstalker in Northernhay

and the river; on a Friday this was my invariable way
home as it took me past the cattle market near Exe
Bridge.   There was a choice of route from there, either
via Coombe Street and James Street to South Street or
via the foul-smelling Commercial Road, with its tannery,
to Quay Lane and Magdalen Street.   I enjoyed all these
variations immensely and missed them when I transferred
to Exeter School.

Those Cathedral Bells!

During these years also I grew more and more conscious
of the cathedral bells: they were a feature of our daily
life and of our festive seasons.   The 8 o'clock bell in
the mornings advised us to hurry, while the 3 o'clock
one, seemingly more peaceful, often warned me of the
need to reach Mother's bank before it closed.   Frequently in holiday time we acted as "runners", since
Mother would delay making up her paying-in slip until
the last possible minute in case a few extra coppers
should be forthcoming.   At Christmas and Easter   there

were prolonged peals from the cathedral tower, less than four hundred yards away: these usually woke us at either 6.00 or 6.30 a.m. They were, of course, quite lovely to hear but I felt, more often than not, a sense of foreboding and a quite strong sense of apprehension and timelessness, although at Christmas these fears were rapidly dispersed as we children examined the stockings and presents which awaited us.

And Now to Exeter School

I do not know exactly when I first decided to leave Hele's. An announcement was made in the spring of 1918 that a scholarship to Exeter School was available for any candidate from Hele's of my age (14). I applied for this, was successful in reaching the required standard and accordingly prepared to change schools in the September of that year. I think the fact that Exeter School had at that time a larger Sixth Form than Hele's, and was therefore more likely to succeed in getting me to university, played a part in my decision.

I am sure few noticed my departure; one member of the staff, I recall, asked me rather acidly why I wanted to leave. On my last day I went to see Mr Snowball; kindly to the last, he expressed regret at my leaving and warned me very plainly on the need to work in the new school. "There will be many there," he said, "who will have no need to carve their own fortunes in the future; with you it is different and work will be the only path to any success."

He was, I found, wrong in his tacit assumption about idleness. Discipline in the pre-Sixth Form year (then called the Remove) was quite strict, while entry to a Sixth Form course depended on a satisfactory standard being reached in the Oxford and Cambridge Joint Board examination taken at the end of that year. In the Sixth Form the drive for scholarships and entry, particularly to the older universities, was acutely felt, perhaps more especially by the day boys and the annual intake of scholars. The senior rugger and cricket teams and the NCOs of the Officers' Training Corps were mostly drawn from the Remove and the boarders. Thus, so far as I could discern, there was none of the free and easy attitude to work which Mr Snowball had feared.

So it was that in mid-September 1918 I found myself walking along Magdalen Road, past St Luke's College and into Exeter School. One or two events remain in my mind in respect of those initial days at the school.

The first of these was the imperative order, of one of the senior boys, to turn up ready for a rugby practice on a certain afternoon. I pointed out that I had played only soccer and had little interest in rugby; this was immediately brushed aside and I was tersely informed, "Every new boy turns up for the first practice."

Well I was obliged to, necessarily, and took my place nervously somewhere in the back line of one of the two sides. The match, for such it was supposed to be, was just about to start when a master on the edge of the pitch noticed that I was wearing spectacles. A hush fell over the whole gathering. In spite of my protests, my glasses were forcibly removed and I was left in a field of misty uncertainty; within seconds I had lost all sense of direction. I never saw a rugby ball, though I knew there must have been one somewhere. After what seemed like a century the "game" ceased, somebody brought back my spectacles and I made an ignominious retreat, in a silence that could almost be felt, to the dressing room. Curiously enough, I was never asked to turn out again for any department of the school's rugby!

In the second place, Mother had in the normal course of events been asked to see the Headmaster at the beginning of term and I had impressed upon her the absolute

necessity of pointing out to him that I was a keen scout and had certain commitments in that direction and that I would therefore unfortunately be unable to join the O.T.C. She promised faithfully to convey my sentiments to Mr England and I awaited her return with calm assurance: this was rapidly shattered. "Unless you have a doctor's certificate," she said, "all boys in the school belong to the Corps. There is no provision for others."

So, to my utter dismay and in the face of bitter unspoken resistance, I found myself kitted out and lining up with the other raw recruits wearing the puttees and so on of the standard uniform and holding very nervously a rifle which seemed to weigh about a hundred pounds. I fear that this particular facet of Exeter School life was a matter of passive resistance throughout the three years I was there.

Wonderful Woodbury Common
I must admit, though, that I did enjoy one day in those three years' unpleasant experience, when the Corps entrained - complete with rifles, five blank rounds each and supplies of food - to take part in "military manoeuvres" on Woodbury Common. This field exercise took place on a remarkably fine day. We marched from Lympstone Station, then broke up into small sections and spread ourselves over the Common to the accompaniment of the occasional blank shot. We passed the time pleasantly in the open air, ate our food in delightful surroundings and all met up once more at Lympstone Station in the late afternoon.

Undoubtedly, however, the main event of those early days at Exeter School was the signing of the Armistice. I remember learning this great news from the excited parent of one of my Hele's School friends while walking down the road a few minutes before 9 o'clock on that November morning. Shortly after the actual signing had taken place the whole school was dismissed for the rest of the day. The occasion was marked in Exeter particularly by the enthusiastic celebrations of the Australian convalescents, who rang the bells of every church in the city into which they were able to gain entry.

Reflections

In bringing these reminiscences to a close I ought to pay a tribute to my parents for their enduring patience and devotion during those early years. In common with the vast majority of ordinary people, they lived for years on the edge of extreme poverty, with Mother frequently confined to her bed by illness.

My own research in the last two or three years has revealed facts which often entirely escaped my notice at the time. For instance, the birth of my youngest brother, Roy, occurred in Oakfield Road some months after my father had gone to Canada; I must have been sent to the Thorverton farm for a week or two during the actual event since I remember nothing whatever about it.

My father returned just before Easter in 1913 and very recently I have discovered an Exeter cemetery record of the burial on 25 November 1913 of a stillborn child born to Mrs Retter of St Mary Major parish, so Mother must have been pregnant again for the 1913 removal from Oakfield Road to East Southernhay; of this, too, I knew nothing.

The last arrival in our family was that of Rosalie Alice, who was born on March 30 in 1916, was baptised privately and died two days later, once more while my father was away, this time in the Forces.

It is not surprising that Mother's health in her later years was so much impaired or, as became clear later, that my father's health too was suffering.

What now seems to me to have been so extraordinary is
that in some way the "middle" members of the family -
Ernest, Phyllis and I - sailed along quite happily
leading our own little lives, serenely unconscious of
the strains and struggles of Mother and my eldest sister
Evelyn.

Yet from her room above the kitchen, Mother planned
ahead and wrote the letters which enabled us to survive.
It was she who decided upon the successive schools her
family should aim at and who pleaded, successfully, her
case for financial help from the Civil Liabilities Tribunal when my father was called into the Forces. At the
same time, while my brothers and sisters helped to keep
the shop from closing she worked to obtain direct
supplies of tobacco and cigarettes from wholesalers
instead of having to rely upon a local firm which, of
course, skimmed off the cream of the profits from their
sale; it took several years to achieve this, but it was
a red letter day for all of us when we were informed
from Bristol that an agent from W D Wills & Co would be
calling shortly at No 52.

When well, Mother took a lively interest in local
affairs; she was an ardent Conservative, attending Ward
meetings whenever an opportunity presented itself. She
was also a mine of information of the genealogical
background of her family.

My father, deeply affectionate and
extremely patient, kept the family in
order and tranquillity. He was a
tremendous physical worker, rising
about six each morning, polishing and
cleaning the shop frontage and
kitchen and so relieving my mother
and Evelyn of as many of the family
chores as he could. I clearly remember the day he was demobilized.

It was not long after the war ended
and the family in the gas-lit kitchen
was just finishing tea when the door
opened and he walked in. There was a
gasp of delight from us all and Mother and the rest of

us clustered happily in greeting around him. It was then that Mother suddenly realised his life in the Services was over; she burst into tears, crying out "Oh Courtney, Courtney, what have you done?" She knew that from that day on all financial support would stop: no Separation Allowance, no army pay for him, no Children's Allowance and no Civil Liabilities Allowance would maintain the household economy. She knew there was no prospect of employment for my father and that once more they were back in the financial struggle of earlier years. She knew that my father could have continued in the army for a few months but instead he had seized the very first opportunity of coming home under the demobilization schedules which had just been published, being immediately released on the grounds that he was required for the care of his family and of the business from which he had been withdrawn in 1915. We children faded out from this scene of wretchedness and left my father to comfort and reassure Mother as best he could.

I think that in those days of mass privation, with no Welfare State in the background, that kind of homecoming must have been the lot of thousands of families. There was to be, in fact, no general answer to the problems thus raised until re-armament began in 1936. I think that the constant worry for his wife and family and the separation from home through his war service led to my father's early death in 1921 at the age of 41; the youngest of his family he was the first to pass away.

After the War the four Gurd children were reunited with their father in Australia. The introduction of refreshments at No 52 for the Australian wounded led in 1918 to my sister Evelyn's engagement to one of them. They were married on 1 January 1919, their first child Courteney was born at Southernhay on 24 September 1919 and in 1920 they departed to set up home in Australia.

Finally, I should add that at the end of the Sixth Form course at Exeter School I proceeded to a degree course in mathematics at what was then Exeter University College. I graduated from there with an external London degree, taking up, just prior to my twenty-first birthday, a teaching post in London.

94

Changes

Apart from the devastation caused by the 1942 German raid, large areas of Exeter were replanned in post-war years to meet modern needs and the ever-increasing use of cars. In what was my particular corner of the city, No 52 Southernhay and the whole block to the bottom of Magdalen Road have been demolished: the cellars, filled in and roughly levelled, provide a few parking places for cars. The other side of Magdalen Road has also been cleared: the "Valiant Soldier", Warne's (the little cycle shop), the greengrocer's, the cobbler's, the dairy and the "Acorn Inn" have all disappeared. From the site of my old home one can now see nothing but the Magdalen Road traffic speeding past.

The lovely fields in Pennsylvania, where we spent so many nights under canvass, are now threatened by Exeter's ever-growing housing devlopment.

While we may lament the passing of so much beauty, we must recall the fortitude required to overcome and survive the manifold disadvantages of the old way of life. My uncle and aunt's comments on too sentimental a memory would probably have been summed up tersely in the words: "Rubbish! You should have tried living then!" A similar remark could well be made in respect of life at No 52 or at any of the adjoining houses: they served their purpose according to the needs of the time at which they were built but the passage of centuries found them unequal to modern demands.

ACKNOWLEDGMENTS

I am indebted to the following:

Westcountry Studies Library, City of Bristol Museum, Mr and Mrs O P Moss, Mrs D Barlow, Mrs A Norris. Mike Williams, Ji▪ Webber, Lil Williamson, Dawlish College, and Chips Barber for photographs and old postcards; Jane Reynolds for all lin◄ drawings.

OTHER OBELISK PUBLICATIONS

AROUND & ABOUT THE HALDON HILLS
Chips Barber, 144 pages, Price £2.50

THE LOST CITY OF EXETER
Chips Barber, 152 pages, Price £2.50

DIARY OF A DARTMOOR WALKER
Chips Barber, 120 pages, Price £2.50

ADVENTURE THROUGH RED DEVON
Raymond B Cattell, 160 pages, Price £2.99

THE TORBAY BOOK
Chips Barber, 176 pages, Price £2.99

If you have any difficulty in obtaining these titles, please write to OBELISK PUBLICATIONS, 22 Causey Gardens, Pinhoe, Exeter. Tel: Exeter 68556. Please add 50p P & P per book.